Atlas, Schmatlas
A Superior Atlas of the World

CRAIG ROBINSON

Abrams Image, New York

For my mum and sister
(Not the same person in case you think my family's weird)

Editor: Deborah Aaronson
Designer: Laura Lindgren
Production Manager: Jacquie Poirier

Library of Congress Cataloging-in-Publication Data
Robinson, Craig, 1970–
   Atlas, schmatlas : a superior atlas of the world / Craig Robinson.
      p. cm.
   Includes bibliographical references.
   ISBN 13: 978-0-8109-9432-4
   ISBN 10: 0-8109-9432-1
   1. World history—Humor. 2. Geography—Humor. I. Title.
   PN6231.H47R63 2007
   900.2'07—dc22   2006039312

Printed and bound in China

10 9 8 7 6 5 4 3 2 1

HNA
harry n. abrams, inc.
a subsidiary of La Martinière Groupe

115 West 18th Street
New York, NY 10011
www.hnabooks.com

"All governments are lying cocksuckers."
Bill Hicks

"L'avenir ne contiendra que ce que nous y mettrons maintenant."
(The future will only contain what we put into it now.)
Graffiti in Paris, May 1968

CONTENTS

A MAP of THE WORLD

Beaufort Sea

Aleutian Islands

Gulf of Alaska

Rocky Mountains

NORTH AMERICA

Hudson Bay

Canadian Shield

Labrador Sea

Great Plains

Appalachian Mts

Gulf of Mexico

Caribbean Sea

PACIFIC OCEAN

EQUATOR

Guiana Highlands

ATLANTIC

Amazon Basin

OCE

SOUTH AMERICA

Planalto de Mato Grosso

Brazilian Highlands

Lake Titicaca

TROPIC OF CAPRICORN

Patagonia

S O U

ANTARCTIC CIRCLE

Weddel Sea

SCALE 1 : 73 000 000

PENNS

0   1   2   3   4   5

0   1   2   3   4

TELLERS

INTRODUCTION

The world is pretty good. It's a big ball floating in space around the sun, just the right distance away for trees, flowers, rivers, and mosquitoes to exist. Humans, too—just like you—live and have done lots of stuff on the planet. Whether you're playing catch at the park, mucking around with your girlfriend behind the bike shed, or thinking of obscene names for your boss while he's telling you to do something you don't want to do, you're a human and you are doing stuff, contributing to the history of mankind.

This atlas is about the oceans, the islands, the continents, and the nations that make up those continents. And it's about the history of those nations that make up those continents. And the animals and plants in those nations that make up those continents.

But most of all, my loves, it's about you.[1]

Wanna find out more? Then, come on! Hop into my book-shaped sports utility vehicle and let's take a ride into Knowledge Canyon.

PS I failed my geography exams at school.[2]

rubbed itself up just right and—BANG!—there was a universe full of planets, stars, moons, and stuff. That's way better than anything David Blaine can do.

Our bit of the universe is the best bit. It's called the Milky Way, and it has eight planets (Pluto got kicked out in 2006 due to cutbacks—the "last in, first out" rule) and a sun and some moons next to some of the planets and some asteroids and some satellites so we can watch live sport and porn.

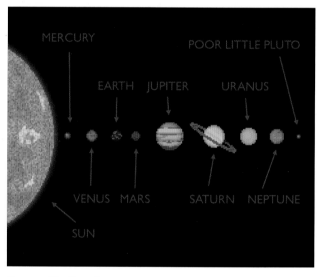

Our sexy lil' milky galaxy.

THE UNIVERSE

The world is at the centre of the universe. Most of the other stuff is pretty superfluous—it's just gas and rocks. The universe was formed about a gazillitrillibillimillion years ago. Before that there was nothing at all. Absolutely nothing. Not even a Starbucks. Then that nothingness

THE EARTH

Although the world might seem like it's the same every day, it's not. Nope, somewhere in the world there's a new McDonald's, and in other places, there are volcanoes getting angry and creating new land.

Underneath our lawns and pavements is something called the crust, and beneath that, something called a mantle, and right in the middle of the planet is the core. The core has two parts: the bit closest to us—the softcore—has got pink stars over its nipples, and the inner core—the hardcore—is showing everything.

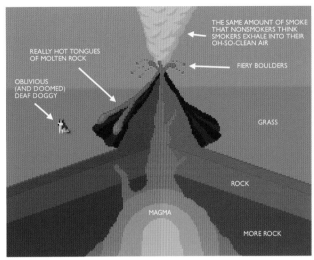

How a volcano works.

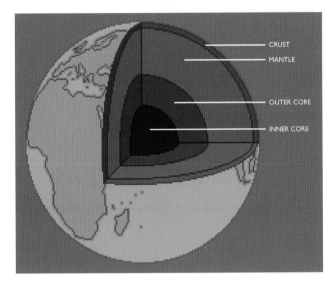

The stuff that makes up our planet.

All this stuff underneath the pavement is slowly moving around. Some bits are moving towards each other and getting all crushed up to make mountains and some bits are moving apart to make places to do bungee jumps.

All of this earth stuff has been studied by geography teachers, and they've worked out that the world used to look like this:

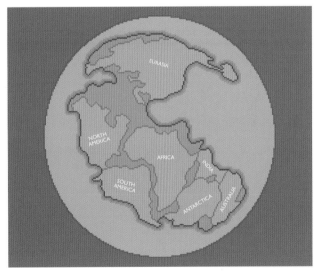

This is how the world used to look. That big supercontinent was called Pangea by the bacteria who were around at the time. That's gotta be quite an impressive ocean on the other side of the globe, huh?

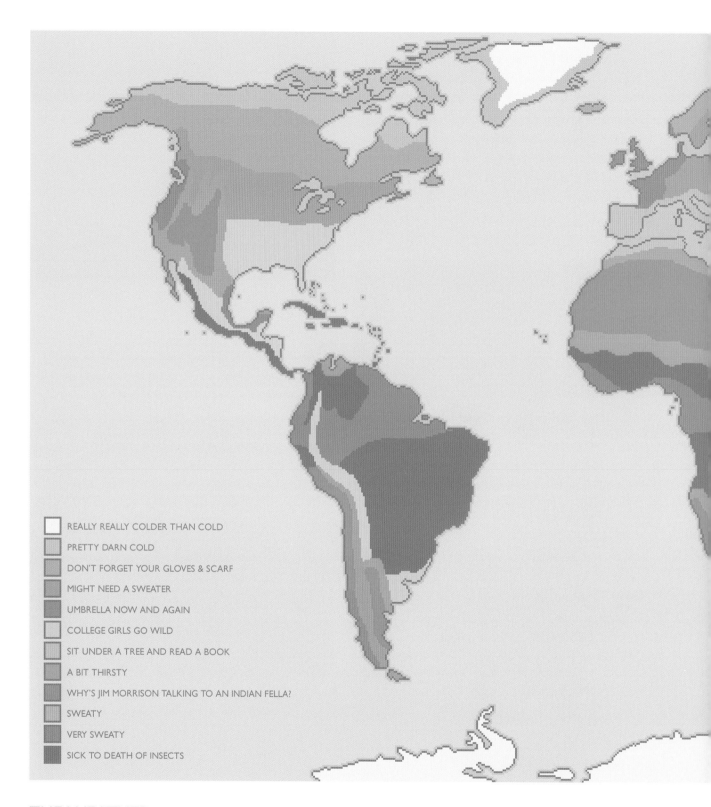

REALLY REALLY COLDER THAN COLD

PRETTY DARN COLD

DON'T FORGET YOUR GLOVES & SCARF

MIGHT NEED A SWEATER

UMBRELLA NOW AND AGAIN

COLLEGE GIRLS GO WILD

SIT UNDER A TREE AND READ A BOOK

A BIT THIRSTY

WHY'S JIM MORRISON TALKING TO AN INDIAN FELLA?

SWEATY

VERY SWEATY

SICK TO DEATH OF INSECTS

THE WEATHER

Most of the stuff that happens on our planet is dictated in one way or another by the weather: if you wanna go skiing, don't go to Chad; if you wanna go surfing, don't go to Chad; if you wanna take some photos of sand, go to Chad.

The climate regions of the world.

LIFE ON EARTH

Is a very good BBC documentary[3] you really should rent because it'll tell you way more than I will, as you'll find by looking at the picture below this paragraph which is just a drawing of some animals.

Look! A flamingo!

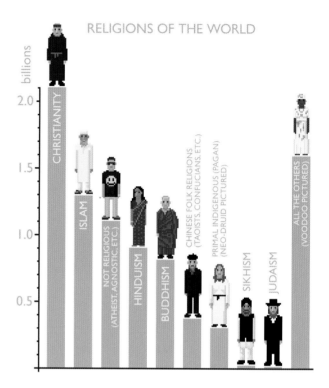

RELIGIONS OF THE WORLD

HUMANS ON EARTH

If you're one of those Christians who believe in that God-did-it-in-six-days joke in the Bible, you might wanna skip this chapter.[4]

Humans like to live in the bits of the planet that aren't too hot or too cold. But some crazy people live in those places anyway, just to prove me wrong. In fact, it was in a hot place—Africa—where we evolved from Neanderthal creatures and left our chimpanzee brothers in the jungle. And over many, many, many generations, people explored farther and farther away from Africa, into western Asia, and around into southern Europe. Some went the other way over to China, over the bit of land that used to connect Russia and Alaska, and down farther and farther into the Americas.

All the movement of these people and the different people they made love with slowly changed how everyone looked. And because they all hung out with their mates all the time, they kinda talked in their own slang, which became new languages. Some started making food between two bits of bread and it was a sandwich, some

made rice with spicy chicken stuff, and others rolled up little bits of fish into pretty shapes and ate them.

Humans also invented something called religion. It's understandable, really; people would see their mums, brothers, or children die and hope that something other than just "death" was happening. So humans had this idea about a god or a bunch of gods. Some gods were helping out with the harvest, some were helping out with bad weather so that school was cancelled, and some gods apparently wanted people to kill themselves in crowded places.

Eventually most people began to cut down on the god stuff, once they realised that actually, nice as going to church is, their quality of life had gotten pretty good without hanging around with the Jesus freaks, and they'd quite like to play golf on Sunday instead.

THE ECONOMY OF THE WORLD

People make the money to pay for being members of golf clubs in many ways. A lot of it has to do with the landscape. Some places grow pigs better, so that's what people there do; some places grow Nike and Adidas shoes, so that's what people there do. So each bit of the world can be used for something special. It's dead good. Most important, though, are the bits of the world with oil underneath the sand. Those bits of the planet are kinda like cash magnets.

THE POLITICAL WORLD

The world has been split up into separate bits by bunches of people who speak the same language and stuff. Some of the borders are natural (coastlines, big rivers,[5] and mountains) and some have evolved over the years. Generally the latter borders came about after a bit of fighting, which is a sport humans seem to enjoy. It involves a few rich blokes telling loads of poor blokes to go and kick the shit out of the poor blokes on the other side who've been told the same stuff by their rich blokes. That's how we've ended up with this world and these countries that we're about to investigate in greater detail.

HOW TO USE THIS ATLAS

Read the words and look at the pictures. Simple.

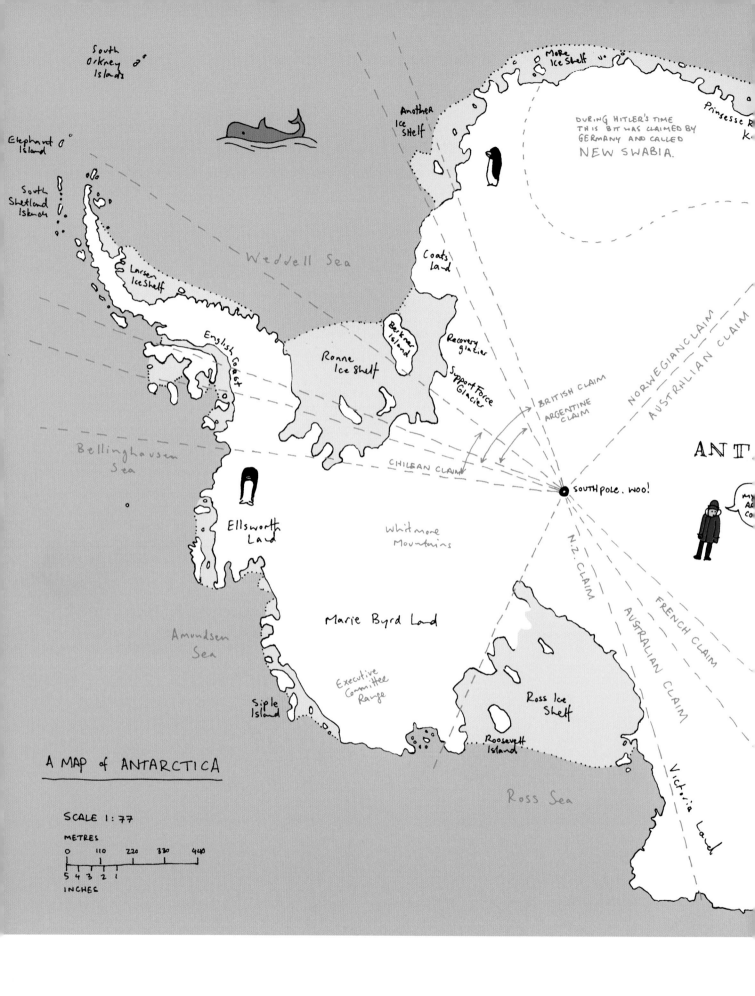

A MAP of ANTARCTICA

SCALE 1:77

METRES

0   110   220   330   440

5 4 3 2 1
INCHES

ANTARCTICA

Let's begin with the icy crap, shall we? Then we can dig into the *real* bits of the planet.

The continent at the bottom of the planet is probably the nicest-shaped continent. It also looks good on maps because it's not a mess of colour and roads and towns.

Antarctica is also the only continent not to ever have had a war take place on it. This unique history was nearly ended in 2003 when polar bears from the Arctic set sail across the Atlantic Ocean to try and take on the penguins. Peace prevailed, though, when the polar bears realised that none of them could sail a ship as they crashed into Iceland.

One of the consequences of the intended attack has been the growth in anti-Arctic feeling within the penguin community. 2005 saw an official visit by a delegation of Emperor penguins to the United Nations requesting that the continent's name be changed from its current Arctic-centric name to Penguinia.

Slices of Antarctica have been claimed by various nations. Australia, New Zealand, France, the UK, Argentina, Chile, and Norway all think they own a bit, but nobody recognises anyone else's claims. One of the few great things that the world's nations have managed to agree on is the 1959 Antarctic Treaty, protecting the continent from military activity, mineral mining, and any attempts to squirt strawberry syrup into the ice to make the world's biggest Slush Puppie.[6]

The penguins gettin' tough with the legislation.

Southern Ocean

The Southern Ocean is the bit of water all around Antarctica. It's the continent's moat, filled with icebergs, and its own current goes round and round and round and round to keep the boatloads of scientists on their toes. It's cold and full of krill, but, on the bright side, there aren't many pirates.

There are loads of islands in the Southern Ocean, most of which are little lumps of rock scattered around the edge of Antarctica, constantly surrounded by ice, so you'd never really know they were islands. But some of the Southern Ocean islands have the sort of names you expect to find in *Mario* games: Deception Island, Dream Island, Elephant Rocks, and Stepping Stones.

But the best names are for islands within the Auckland Islands group, south of New Zealand (which, depending on your definition of where one ocean ends and another begins, might actually be in the Pacific): Fabulous Island, Masked Island, Shag Rock, Shoe Island, and the island that the glass-half-empty part of me would most like to visit, Disappointment Island.

ARCTIC

This is the cold bit at the top of the world. There's not much land there; it's mostly a big ice cube. In the middle of the Arctic is the North Pole. It marks the world's most northernliest barbershop where polar bears can go for a trim in the summer and rich explorers can stop by to read some out-of-date magazines and have a cup of tea.

In summer it's always sunny. All day long. In winter it's always dark. All day long. That must be quite annoying. All year long.

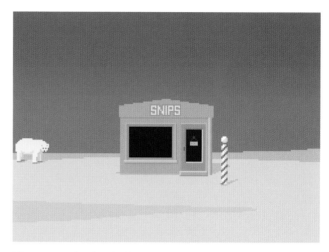

The most northernliest barber shop in the world.

 GREENLAND

OFFICIAL NAME: Kalaallit Nunaat/Grønland (Greenland)
AREA: 2,166,086 sq km
POPULATION: 56,375 (2005 est.)
CAPITAL: Nuuk (Godthåb)
LANGUAGE(S): Greenlandic, Danish

Greenland, long thought to just be a fictional country from Peter Høeg's book *Miss Smilla's Feeling for Snow,* is actually the world's largest island. Most of it is covered with ice, and is, therefore, completely useless. The few people who live here tend to wear coats a lot and like shrimp more than Forrest Gump's mate.

Greenland[7] has the best flag in the whole wide world.[8]

 SVALBARD

OFFICIAL NAME: Svalbardoohitsbløødycoldyåbastård
AREA: 62,049 sq km
POPULATION: 2,756 (2004 est.)
CAPITAL: Longyearbyen
LANGUAGE(S): Norwegian

Invented by a disgruntled Icelandic mayor, Svalbard began life also being called Iceland. Thinking he could run an Iceland better without all the pesky meddling of the locals, he built Iceland (the Svalbard one), and began siphoning off tourists from Iceland (the proper one)

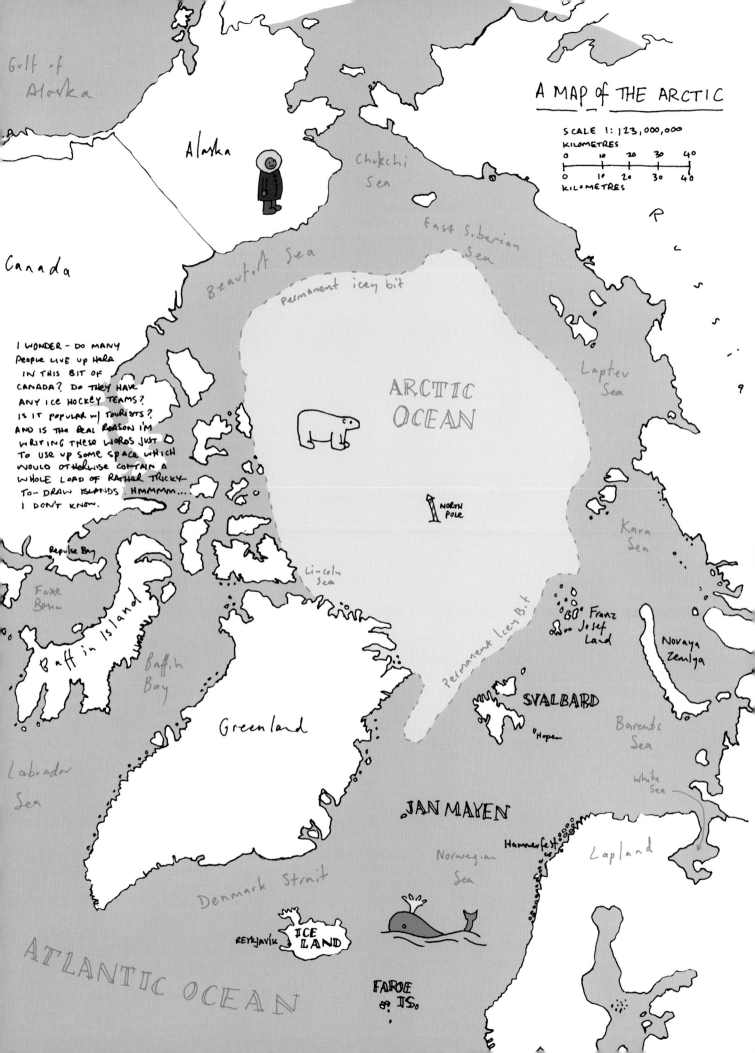

with deliberately ambiguous advertising. His rather crude geysers—made of watering cans attached to pumps—were no match for the real Iceland's geysers and when Iceland (the real one) threatened to sue, he changed the name of his Iceland to Nordaustlandet, anchored it next to a couple of other islands, and drank himself to death on a glacier.

 JAN MAYEN

OFFICIAL NAME: Jan Mayen
AREA: 373 sq km
POPULATION: 18 (2006 est.)
CAPITAL: That snowy bit
LANGUAGE(S): Norwegian

Jan Mayen was a Dutch fisherman. He froze to death when he fell into the North Atlantic Ocean trying to catch a strong and stubborn whale. His mates couldn't be arsed to drag him back on the boat so they left him. Snow landed on him, some birds pooped on him, and slowly he grew to be island-sized. Nowadays a bunch of Norwegian weathermen and women work there. Jan Mayen has no professional football league.

NORTH AMERICA

North America looks like when you've got a new bottle of ketchup and your burger's getting cold and you shake the bottle really hard to get the tomato-y goodness out and it splatters all over the plate, ruining your meal.

For the puerile minds out there, three parts of North America look like penises: Florida, Manhattan, and Lake Michigan.

 CANADA

OFFICIAL NAME: Canada
AREA: 9,984,670 sq km
POPULATION: 31,946,400 (2004 est.)
CAPITAL: Ottawa
LANGUAGE(S): English, French

This is the bit of North America that the English didn't want, agreeing as they did with Voltaire that it was nothing more than "a few acres of snow."

So France snapped it up, then let the Queen of England have some of it as long as she agreed to make the toilet signs in French too.

These days the primary function of Canada is to be the word that more cultured Americans use when asked by Europeans where they come from.

An everyday scene in downtown Toronto.

SAINT-PIERRE and MIQUELON

OFFICIAL NAME: Saint-Pierre-et-Miquelon (Saint-Pierre and Miquelon)
AREA: 242 sq km
POPULATION: 6,316 (1999 census)
CAPITAL: Saint-Pierre
LANGUAGE(S): French

A Frenchy outpost, right next to Canada, that you possibly wouldn't notice on a map. France keeps hold of these couple of islands just to make sure that people in Canada keep on talking in their language. The president of Saint-Pierre and Miquelon is probably Gérard Depardieu.

UNITED STATES

OFFICIAL NAME: United States of America
AREA: 9,522,057 sq km
POPULATION: 293,655,404 (2004 est.)
CAPITAL: Washington, DC
LANGUAGE(S): No official language (as first language: English 82.11%, Spanish 10.71%, Native American languages 0.15%)

The United States of America is, as the name suggests, a bunch of states that are united in the northern part of the Americas. The United States was formed when some Europeans got lost on their way to China and decided that they couldn't be arsed to go home. At first they thought they were alone but soon found some natives who lived in wigwams who'd sat around twiddling their thumbs for, like, *ever*, waiting for people to arrive so they could play Cowboys and Indians properly. Little did they know that they'd get their arses kicked royally. With their tails between their legs, the natives trundled off to the boring desert-y bit of the country and built some casinos.

The Europeans, meanwhile, set about dragging loads of African fellas across the ocean to make them do all the hard work involved in building a nation, while they just lounged around on the beach drinking Manhattans and peanut butter milkshakes.

Several generations after these events, after the original European settlers had children, and their children had children, and *their* children had children, the settlers started to feel like they weren't European any more, and got a bit bored of having to sing "God Save The King" every day. So they invented a new song to sing at school

every day called "Surfin' USA" and the British monarch slunk away like a sad puppy after a scolding.

Free of the king and his la-de-da British ways, the Americans decided that they'd have a president instead, one that wasn't part of a rich family where fathers and sons ruled the nation and just helped out their rich mates.

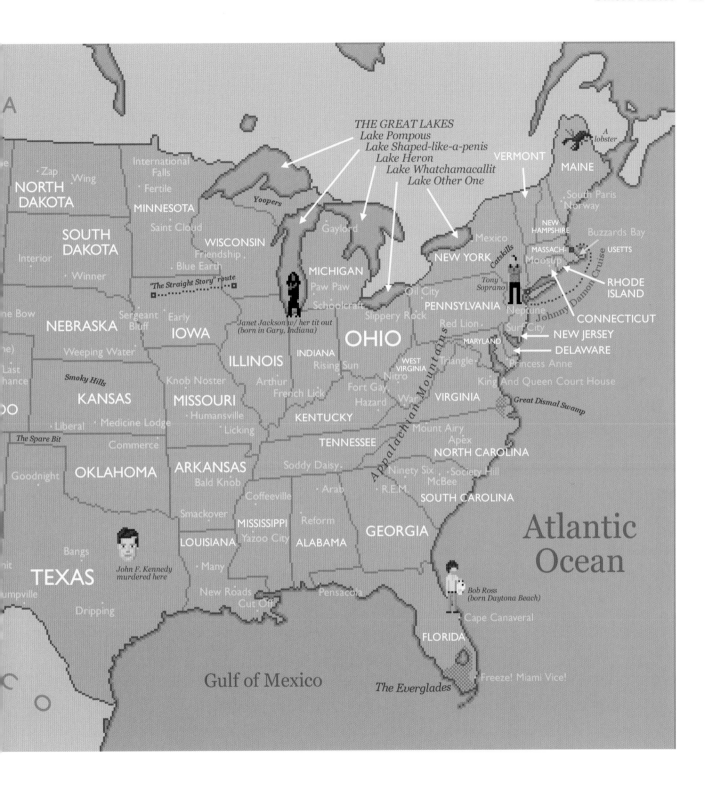

THE GREAT LAKES
Lake Pompous
Lake Shaped-like-a-penis
Lake Heron
Lake Whatchamacallit
Lake Other One

BERMUDA

OFFICIAL NAME: Bermuda
AREA: 53 sq km
POPULATION: 62,059 (2000 census)
CAPITAL: Hamilton
LANGUAGE(S): English

Bermuda has more golf courses per capita than any other country in the world. It makes my brain hurt to think of all the crap jokes businessmen must have made about their bad shots and the Bermuda Triangle.

MEXICO

OFFICIAL NAME: Estados Unidos Mexicanos (United Mexican States)
AREA: 1,964,375 sq km
POPULATION: 97,483,412 (2000 census)
CAPITAL: Mexico City
LANGUAGE(S): Spanish and loads of native languages

Mexico, a nation with a hard-ass eagle eating a snake on its flag, has a long and impressive history. The Olmec civilisation invented the lottery, the Teotihuacan had the world's largest city in 500 AD, the Mayans created advanced political order, the Toltec invented the chicken-and-the-egg joke, and the Aztecs invented gold. All was peachy, then the Spanish arrived. With the use of a crude mask made of cardboard and finger paint, Hernán Cortés dressed up as the Aztec god Quetzalcoatl to fool the Aztec leader Moctezuma II. "Ha! Ha!" said Cortés, whipping off his mask, "I have fooled you with my Iberian cunning!" He then took over Tenochtitlan and built Mexico City on top of it and decreed that all men shall wear their moustaches droopy and make their hats bigger.

Corruption, as in many countries around the world, has been a problem in Mexico. Once upon a time a rich man called Antonio paid the princely sum of three thousand pesos and a truck full of eggs for the pronunciation of his country to be changed to "Mehico" just because he didn't like the sound of the letter X.

Work recently began on a 1,900-mile barrier on the border with the United States with the hope of keeping Spring Break teenagers and macho idiots on stag weekends out of Mexico. The barrier will be guarded by a masked army of *luchadores* under orders to smack down anyone trying to illegally enter Mexico.[9]

TV sitcom character El Chavo del 8, luchadores El Santo and Blue Demon, football hero Hugo Sanchez, the coolest man on the planet Subcomandante Marcos, former president Vicente Fox, artists Diego Rivera and Frida Kahlo, revolutionary chap Emiliano Zapata, and Aztec ruler Moctezuma II.

CENTRAL AMERICA

Technically, it's part of North America, but if you include Mexico (which the UN does in its subregional description of Central America), it looks like a spit-roasted deer's leg, half-eaten by a king. This region of the Americas is the bit where your dreams might be realised if you fancy a career as a CIA-backed military dictator.

BELIZE

OFFICIAL NAME: Belize
AREA: 22,965 sq km
POPULATION: 282,600 (2004 est.)
CAPITAL: Belmopan
LANGUAGE(S): English

The old Mayan people who used to populate Belize graciously allowed themselves to be slaughtered so that fat modern-day tourists could slurp cold Cokes on the ruins of their fancy old buildings and get a feeling of being in touch with the natives that their forefathers slaughtered.[10]

GUATEMALA

OFFICIAL NAME: República de Guatemala (Republic of Guatemala)
AREA: 109,117 sq km
POPULATION: 11,237,196 (2002 census)
CAPITAL: Guatemala City
LANGUAGE(S): Spanish

Hi! Welcome to the CIA Show! Yes! Here we see the unmistakable boot-print of American foreign policy! Marvel at democratically elected governments being over-thrown because the U.S. doesn't like 'em! Gasp as anyone disagreeing with the U.S. is shut up—*permanently!* Go gung ho "Let's Roll!" when the U.S.-supported military dictatorship kills around two hundred thousand Guatemalans! And praise God for those cheap bananas in your kitchen!

 EL SALVADOR

OFFICIAL NAME: República de El Salvador (Republic of El Salvador)
AREA: 21,042 sq km
POPULATION: 6,757,408 (2004 est.)
CAPITAL: San Salvador
LANGUAGE(S): Spanish

El Salvador is named in honour of Bono.[11]

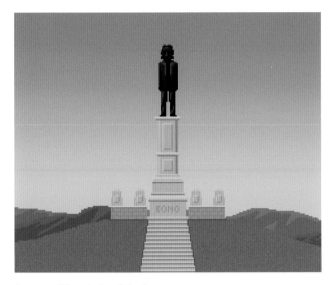

A statue of Bono in San Salvador.

 HONDURAS

OFFICIAL NAME: República de Honduras (Republic of Honduras)
AREA: 112,492 sq km
POPULATION: 6,535,344 (2001 census)
CAPITAL: Tegucigalpa
LANGUAGE(S): Spanish

Hondurans were so devastated by the cancellation of *Baywatch Nights* that they named the equally devastating Hurricane Mitch after Hasselhoff's character.

 NICARAGUA

OFFICIAL NAME: República de Nicaragua (Republic of Nicaragua)
AREA: 130,373 sq km
POPULATION: 5,626,492 (2004 est.)
CAPITAL: Managua
LANGUAGE(S): Spanish

Sitting in his swanky office one evening, Ronald Reagan was humming along to the George Benson hit "Greatest Love of All" that was on the radio. Turning to his mate from the CIA, he said, "I, too, believe that children are the future."

"Which children, sir?" replied the black-hearted fellow.

"The ones in Nicaragua, my man," chortled the president, as he signed a piece of paper condemning many of those children to be orphans and sold weapons to Iran to fund the Nicaraguan anti-communist guerrilla organisation, the Contras.[12]

They both lit cigars and laughed like Satan for many a minute. Reagan was so excited by his dastardliness that he even did a little bit of wee in his pants.

 COSTA RICA

OFFICIAL NAME: República de Costa Rica (Republic of Costa Rica)
AREA: 51,100 sq km
POPULATION: 4,159,757 (2004 est.)
CAPITAL: San José
LANGUAGE(S): Spanish

Costa Rica has no army. Don't they realise they'll never have a military *junta* without one and never become an easy Latin-American banana republic cliché for us westerners?

 PANAMA

OFFICIAL NAME: República de Panamá (Republic of Panama)
AREA: 75,040 sq km
POPULATION: 3,172,360 (2004 est.)
CAPITAL: Panama City
LANGUAGE(S): Spanish

Panama is an entirely man-made nation. Once upon a time, North and South America were completely separate with a big Panama-shaped gap allowing ships safe passage from California to Florida. Then in 1903, some Colombian bloke had an idea: Let's build a country

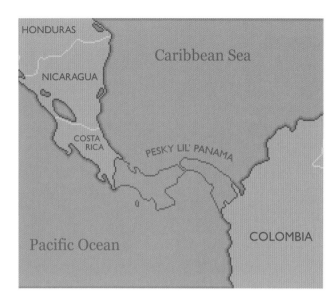

here and make a really thin bit of water for ships to go through, then we can charge them *mucho dollar* to get through. "Good idea!" said everyone else, as they shovelled sand into the ocean.

CARIBBEAN

You know when you've overslept a little and you're rushing to drink your coffee and eat your cornflakes before you run out to get the bus? And you don't have time to finish the bowl of cornflakes, and as you grab your briefcase, you accidentally knock the bowl off the table and it goes all over the floor? That's what the Caribbean islands look like.

The Caribbean Sea is situated in that bit between North and South America, and there's more than seven thousand islands for hurricanes to fuck with.

 THE BAHAMAS

OFFICIAL NAME: The Commonwealth of The Bahamas
AREA: 13,939 sq km
POPULATION: 303,611 (2000 census)
CAPITAL: Nassau
LANGUAGE(S): English

In 1492, after two-and-a-bit months sailing across the Atlantic Ocean and desperately in need of a good poo, Christopher Columbus spotted land—what is now known as the Bahamas.

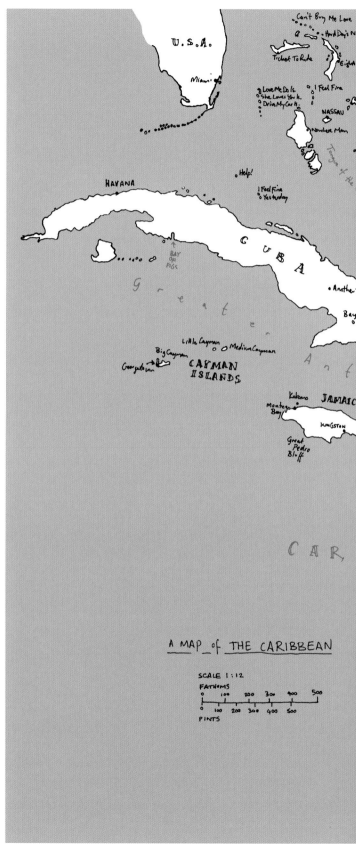

A MAP of THE CARIBBEAN

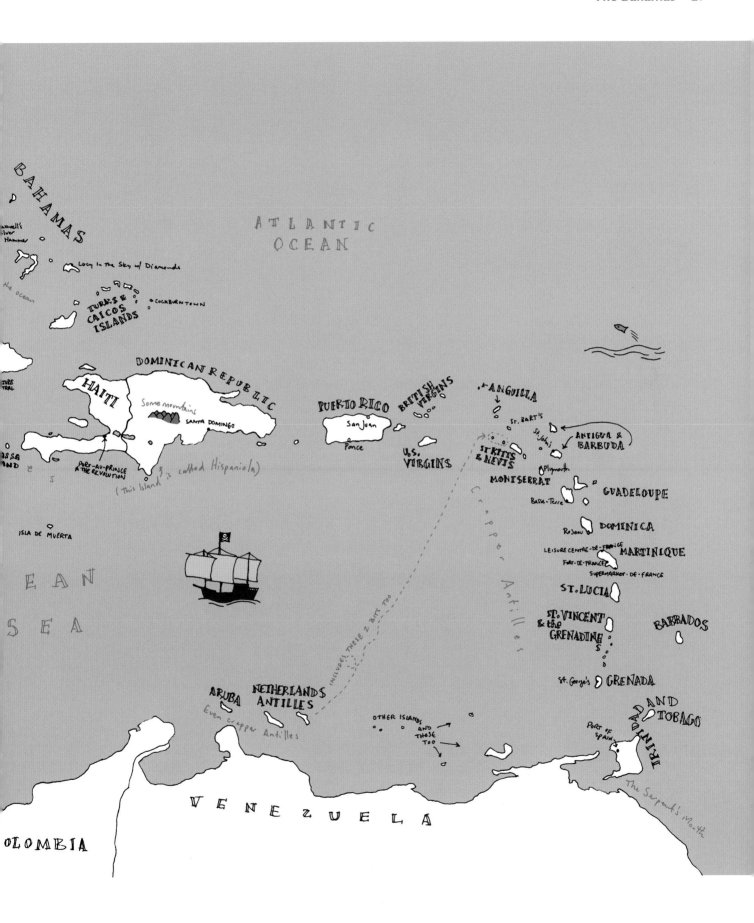

BAHAMAS

ATLANTIC OCEAN

Maxwell's Silver Hammer

Lucy in the Sky w/ Diamonds

the ocean

TURKS & CAICOS ISLANDS

COCKBURN TOWN

DOMINICAN REPUBLIC

HAITI

Some mountains

SANTA DOMINGO

PORT-AU-PRINCE & THE REVOLUTION

(This Island is called Hispaniola)

PUERTO RICO

San Juan

Ponce

BRITISH VIRGINS

U.S. VIRGINS

ANGUILLA

St. BART'S

St. John's

ANTIGUA & BARBUDA

ST KITTS & NEVIS

Plymouth

MONTSERRAT

Basse-Terre

GUADELOUPE

Crapper Antilles

Roseau

DOMINICA

LEISURE CENTRE-DE-FRANCE

Fort-de-France

SUPERMARKET-DE-FRANCE

MARTINIQUE

ST. LUCIA

ST. VINCENT & the GRENADINES

BARBADOS

St. George's

GRENADA

ISLA DE MUERTA

EAN

SEA

INCLUDES THESE 2 BITS TOO

ARUBA

NETHERLANDS ANTILLES

Even crapper Antilles

OTHER ISLANDS

AND THOSE TOO

PORT OF SPAIN

TRINIDAD AND TOBAGO

The Serpent's Mouth

VENEZUELA

OLOMBIA

"Look! It's the New World," he exclaimed. "Bring me some toilet paper, Rodrigo, I'm gonna go behind those bushes as soon as we land."

After he'd done his business, he and Rodrigo went for a walk.

"This is nice, innit, Rodrigo?" he said.

"Aye, it's right pretty, sir," said Rodrigo. "'You reckon those blokes over there sell ice cream? I could murder a mint choc-chip cornet."

"Let's go find out!" Columbus shouted with a fancy flourish of the arm.

They walked towards the savages smiling.

"Hello there," said Chris. "Where the devil are we?"

"All right there," said one of the native Taíno folks. "This island is Guanahani!"

"Guana-*what?* That's quite a mouthful. Let's change the name to San Salvador, eh?" insisted Chris.

Rodrigo furiously tapped on Columbus's shoulder, then whispered, "Ask them about the ice cream!"

Chris asked but the locals had no ice cream. So Chris and Rodrigo bid them farewell and went off to Cuba to buy some Che Guevara T-shirts.

The natives' idyllic Pre-Columbian era was over. Within months of Columbus's visit, their beaches were full of hotels and car rental shops.

 TURKS and CAICOS ISLANDS

OFFICIAL NAME: Turks and Caicos Islands
AREA: 430 sq km
POPULATION: 19,500 (2003 est.)
CAPITAL: Cockburn Town
LANGUAGE(S): English

Geographically part of the Bahamas; politically part of dear old Blighty.

There's only one Goth amongst the nearly twenty thousand Turks and Caicos Island citizens. She is seventeen-year-old Susie Gruftie and she lives in Balfour Town on the Salt Cay Island. The poor little lamb's all alone with her Xmal Deutschland and Covenant tapes, and it gets mighty hot with all the hair. If only she knew that in Bambarra on the Middle Caicos Island there is a fairly moody teenage boy who quite likes the odd Marilyn Manson song; maybe she could turn him to the dark side....

Susie. All alone. And probably a bit sweaty.

 CUBA

OFFICIAL NAME: República de Cuba (Republic of Cuba)
AREA: 110,861 sq km
POPULATION: 11,243,400 (2002 est.)
CAPITAL: Havana
LANGUAGE(S): Spanish

Discovered by Columbus while looking for a shop that sold Buena Vista Social Club CDs. He stocked up on duty-free cigars, too.

After Cuba[13] gained independence from Spain with help from the United States, Cubans decided that they liked a spot of communism with their breakfast coffee, and Fidel Castro took over as president.

The Americans weren't happy about this and I'm really trying to resist some porcine-related Bay of Pigs joke here.

Since the fall of the Soviet Union, Cuba has suffered economically, except when it comes to selling cigars to bad guys or ostentatiously rich blokes in American films.

While a hero to some, Castro is also pretty unpopular with a lot of Cubans, Cuban exiles, and human rights groups. Oddly, considering the ill feeling towards Castro, the Americans decided to help him out by shifting the focus of human rights abuses occurring on Cuban soil to their own rented bit of land, Guantánamo Bay.

As this book goes to print, it would seem that Fidel Castro is pretty ill. Who knows if he'll be around when you—yes, you—are reading these words? If he has passed away while this book was being printed, please reread the preceding paragraph with all verb tenses changed from present to past.

CAYMAN ISLANDS

OFFICIAL NAME: Cayman Islands
AREA: 260 sq km
POPULATION: 44,270 (2005 est.)
CAPITAL: George Town
LANGUAGE(S): English

One of the best known tax havens in the world, mainly because the banks are run by parrots and turtles who pretend not to speak English when the FBI turns up wanting to have a look around. It also helps that they employ crocodiles as security guards.

JAMAICA

OFFICIAL NAME: Jamaica
AREA: 10,991 sq km
POPULATION: 2,607,600 (2001 census)
CAPITAL: Kingston
LANGUAGE(S): English

Sick of living out of his suitcase on his trips, Christopher Columbus picked Jamaica to be his family's estate when he arrived there in 1494. He put in an Olympic-size pool, a fountain, a double garage with remote control doors, and some rather gaudy statues of lions by the gate.

A couple of hundred years later, when the Brits had grabbed the island from the Spanish, they started bringing loads of slaves over from Africa to harvest all the sugar plants because the fancy British folk loved sticky cakes and sweet, sweet tea.

One day, the Brits noticed they were massively outnumbered by the slaves and slipped out the back door, leaving Jamaica as an independent nation. (They kept Queen Elizabeth II as their monarch though, because they liked her jewels.)

Once independence was achieved, Jamaicans set about inventing some music that would be incredibly influential in many splendid ways. Sadly though, it also influenced some misguided white students to think that dreadlocks would suit them.

A bunch of famous Jamaicans: singer and model and actress Grace Jones, reggae dude King Tubby, fancy hat wearer Marcus Garvey, student poster icon Bob Marley, Lee "Scratch" Perry, basketball player Patrick Ewing, and Jamaican-born Canadian runner Ben Johnson.

NAVASSA ISLAND

OFFICIAL NAME: Navassa Island
AREA: 5.2 sq km
POPULATION: some birds
CAPITAL: some nests
LANGUAGE(S): Ploppy

A big pile of seagull poo owned by the United States.

HAITI

OFFICIAL NAME: Repiblik Dayti/République d'Haïti (Republic of Haiti)
AREA: 27,700 sq km
POPULATION: 7,491,762 (1997 est.)
CAPITAL: Port-au-Prince
LANGUAGE(S): Haitian Creole, French

Haiti makes up the western third of the island of Hispaniola, an island it shares with the Dominican Republic. In 1804, it became the second country in the Americas, after the United States, to achieve independence.

Claimed by that man Columbus in 1492, Hispaniola's Taíno and Arawak people were soon forced to collect gold for Chris to take back to Spain. Columbus would chop off the hands of any of them who didn't collect enough. Nice.

Two hundred years later, the French arrived with a bunch of African slaves and had a jolly old time for a century until some voodoo started the Haitian Revolution.

"Sacre bleu!" said Pierre. "That voodoo that you do makes me feel blue, like a snooker cue attached to a canoe made of bamboo going up my poo… hole."

The twentieth century has been a fairly turbulent time in Haitian history. Invaded and occupied by the U.S. for nearly twenty years, Haiti was then ruled from 1957 to

1986 by father and son dictatorial tag-team, "Papa Doc" and "Baby Doc" Duvalier. Jean-Bertrand Aristide was elected in 1991, then deposed in a coup, then returned to power after control by a military *junta* and another U.S. occupation, and once again overthrown in 2004.

During this time, Haitian-born Wyclef Jean released some records just to make things worse.

DOMINICAN REPUBLIC

OFFICIAL NAME: República Dominicana (Dominican Republic)
AREA: 48,671 sq km
POPULATION: 8,230,722 (2002 census)
CAPITAL: Santo Domingo
LANGUAGE(S): Spanish

Blah blah blah Hispaniola blah blah blah Christopher Columbus blah blah blah Haiti became French blah blah blah. A bit later the Spanish let the Dominican Republic have its independence. In 1916, though, the U.S. occupied the country for eight years, setting up baseball-player farms where players are grown to this day.

(l-r) Some of the Dominican Republic's finest baseball players: Robinson Canó, Bartolo Colón, Vladimir Guerrero, Pedro Martínez, David Ortiz, Albert Pujols, Alfonso Soriano, Sammy Sosa, Miguel Tejada, and Juan Uribe.

PUERTO RICO

OFFICIAL NAME: Estado Libre Asociado de Puerto Rico/ Commonwealth of Puerto Rico
AREA: 9,104 sq km
POPULATION: 3,879,000 (2003 est.)
CAPITAL: San Juan
LANGUAGE(S): Spanish, English

Let's play a game. Take the map of the Caribbean islands that I've drawn, and arrange doggie treats on the kitchen floor in roughly the same configuration as the islands. Now let your dog into the room, sit back, and watch what happens.

Done it? Fun, huh? That, my friends, was your dog playing the role of Christopher Columbus in the fifteenth century, snaffling up every speck of land on his journey.

Puerto Rico was one of those islands.

The readers of *Island & Atoll Monthly* recently voted Puerto Rico as the "World's Most Boringly Shaped Island."

BRITISH VIRGIN ISLANDS

OFFICIAL NAME: British Virgin Islands
AREA: 153 sq km
POPULATION: 21,730 (2002 est.)
CAPITAL: Road Town
LANGUAGE(S): English

This neighbour of the U.S. Virgin Islands is an overseas territory of the United Kingdom. The capital, Road Town, was named for the numerous thoroughfares that ran through the town. Tourism is the main source of income on the islands. Visitors frequently go to places of natural beauty such as Lava Mountain, Tree Forest, Sea Beach, and the beautiful coral reefs near Coral Reef Bay.

The currency of the British Virgin Islands is called the Cash Money.

U.S. VIRGIN ISLANDS

OFFICIAL NAME: United States Virgin Islands
AREA: 352 sq km
POPULATION: 124,778 (2003 est.)
CAPITAL: Charlotte Amalie
LANGUAGE(S): English

Tourism was once the primary economic activity on this group of islands, but since the late 1990s it has been overtaken by Internet pornography Web sites. Such is the magnitude of this business that the U.S. Virgin Islands, a dependency of the United States of America, is going through a crisis comparable to the deforestation of the Amazon. Virgin girls are being deflowered at an alarming rate. Indeed, the country has recently added redheaded teens to the World Conservation Union's list of endangered species. Only three virgin redheaded teens are known to exist, and the only Virgin Islands male carrying the dysfunctional variant of the MC1R protein gene (thought to be responsible for causing red hair) has publicly stated that he prefers brunettes.

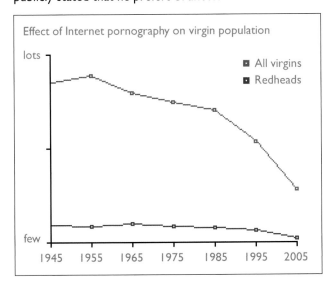

ANGUILLA

OFFICIAL NAME: Anguilla
AREA: 91 sq km
POPULATION: 12,800 (2002 est.)
CAPITAL: The Valley
LANGUAGE(S): English

There's a place in Anguilla called Blowing Point. That's where horny Anguillans congregate to... I don't need to finish this sentence, do I?[14]

NETHERLANDS ANTILLES

OFFICIAL NAME: Nederlandse Antillen (Netherlands Antilles)
AREA: 960 sq km
POPULATION: 219,958 (2005 est.)
CAPITAL: Willemstad
LANGUAGE(S): Dutch

You know when you're walking along, you involuntarily swing your arms back and forth, and if you try and keep your arms still, straight down by your side, it feels weird, right? Well, that's how they walk here.

SAINT KITTS and NEVIS

OFFICIAL NAME: Federation of Saint Christopher and Nevis
AREA: 269 sq km
POPULATION: 45,884 (2001 census)
CAPITAL: Basseterre
LANGUAGE(S): English

Saint Kitts and Nevis, the smallest nation in the Western Hemisphere, is an independent Commonwealth Realm. Every year since achieving autonomy in 1967, there's been an annual bragging competition between the islands, the Saint Kitts and Nevis Chatter Championship. On the face of it it's just a bit of fun, but over the years, a fierce rivalry has developed, with Nevis having won thirty-nine trophies, and Saint Kitts just one.

Nevis's dominance is due to bragging about Lord Nelson marrying a Nevisian lass, Fanny Nesbit, in 1787. Saint Kitts can't really argue with that, especially when Nevisian speaker Joshua Rosen recited Nelson's full name in a pineapple-tinged baritone (Lord Horatio Nelson, Viscount and Baron Nelson of the Nile and of Burnham

Thorpe in the County of Norfolk, Baron Nelson of the Nile and of Hillborough in the said County, Knight of the Most Honourable Order of the Bath, Vice Admiral of the White Squadron of the Fleet, Commander in Chief of His Majesty's Ships and Vessels in the Mediterranean, Duke of Bronte in Sicily, Knight Grand Cross of the Sicilian Order of St. Ferdinand and of Merit, Member of the Ottoman Order of the Crescent, and Knight Grand Commander of the Order of St. Joachim).

Saint Kitts's sole victory came in 1981, when the Nevisian speaker was mysteriously struck down with food poisoning, forcing an inexperienced boy to compete. Saint Kitts's speaker Keith McColl claimed to have invented the Rubik's Cube,[15] impressing the judges to no end.

ANTIGUA and BARBUDA

OFFICIAL NAME: Antigua and Barbuda
AREA: 441 sq km
POPULATION: 75,741 (2001 census)
CAPITAL: Saint John's
LANGUAGE(S): English

Back in 1987, a gang of entertainment lawyers in Los Angeles were making calls to the bigwigs of several Caribbean islands. They were taking bids from the tourism councils to be included in the forthcoming Beach Boys song "Kokomo."

All but one slot of the song had been decided, but the most prominent position—the first location to be mentioned in the chorus—was still being argued about. Barbuda was the favourite to take this prime slot, but a late and massive bid from Aruba dislodged Barbuda from the song. Tourism in Barbuda nosedived. Tourism in Aruba did the opposite type of dive. Since the song reached number one on the *Billboard* chart on November 5, 1988, Barbudans have commemorated the event annually by burning an effigy of Beach Boy Mike Love on a bonfire.

MONTSERRAT

OFFICIAL NAME: Montserrat
AREA: 102 sq km
POPULATION: 9,341 (2005 est.)
CAPITAL: Plymouth (although the de facto capital is Brades because a lot of Plymouth was buggered up by the eruption of a volcano in 1997)
LANGUAGE(S): English

The locals were out on the streets. "I want my MTV!" they shouted. "No!" replied the governor, "the BBC will do you just fine."

But the locals persisted, sick as they were of just watching British telly programmes. A few miles away, Mark Knopfler, of the popular rock group Dire Straits, was playing Connect Four with Sting over a nice glass of iced tea on the gold-plated terrace of Air Studios. Sting started to repeat the crowd's echoey chant in a slightly haunting manner, strangely reminiscent of the melodic line of the Police's hit song "Don't Stand So Close to Me." "Hold on," said Knopfler, fingers a-bristlin' with finger-pickin' creativity, "I'll get my guitar." And so it came to be: "Money for Nothing." And your chicks for free.

It was a good fifteen years before Montserrat got its MTV, because, amongst other things, Hurricane Hugo messed things up real bad in 1989. When MTV did arrive

Sting and Mark Knopfler taking a break from their Connect Four marathon to listen to the locals chant for their MTV.

most of the islanders were disappointed to find that MTV no longer showed DeBarge, Timex Social Club, and Colonel Abrams videos—just shows about tarting up old cars, *The Osbournes* (which they quite liked, as it goes), and Spring Break-ing idiot students eating dog poo from the inside of a rotting whale carcass for $70 in front of a delirious crowd of their drunken peers.

"We no longer want our MTV!" they cried. "Make your bloody minds up," said the slightly irked governor, rolling her eyes and silently mouthing the word "wankers" to her colleague, the chief minister.

 GUADELOUPE

OFFICIAL NAME: Départment de la Guadeloupe (Department of Guadeloupe)
AREA: 1,705 sq km
POPULATION: 422,496 (1999 census)
CAPITAL: Basse-Terre
LANGUAGE(S): French

Another island found by Christopher Columbus on his second trip in 1493. Chris and his mate Rodrigo pulled up on the beach of Pointe Tarare.

"Chris! Come here, look at this!" cried Rodrigo.

Columbus joined Rodrigo on the beach and stared, eyes agog, mouth a-open. Standing in front of them there were loads of natives playing volleyball. All in the nip. Naked! Nude!

"Well, I never!" exclaimed Christopher.

"Indeed! Shall we, er, y'know, join them?" asked Rodrigo with a lascivious grin and fingers crossed behind his back.

"No, we shall not! It's not very Catholic, is it? Besides, I'm busting for a dump. Here, hold my rucksack while I nip behind those rocks."

Five hundred years later, and now a *département d'outre-mer* of France, Guadeloupe still has a nudist beach at Pointe Tarare. In fact, it's the oldest one in the world. If you fancy seeing famous people with no clothes on, though, head up to Saint-Barthélemy: That's where they all hang out, even though they know full well that those boats in the distance are full of paparazzi.

 DOMINICA

OFFICIAL NAME: Commonwealth of Dominica
AREA: 739 sq km
POPULATION: 71,183 (1991 census)
CAPITAL: Roseau
LANGUAGE(S): English

Christopher Columbus landed here on his second trip to the New World in 1493 and would've included it as a territory of the Dominican Republic had he not run out of ink when he was writing it on the map.

 MARTINIQUE

OFFICIAL NAME: Départment de la Martinique (Department of Martinique)
AREA: 1,128 sq km
POPULATION: 381,427 (1999 census)
CAPITAL: Fort-de-France
LANGUAGE(S): French

Guess who discovered this place? That's right. On his fourth and final holiday to the New World in 1502, Christopher Columbus found Martinique.

As they got off the boat, his companion Rodrigo noticed that Columbus seemed glum.

"What's wrong, mate?" asked Rodrigo, putting his arm around Columbus and feeling a frisson of excitement in his pants.

"I dunno, my dear Rod," said Chris. "I'm just not as excited as I used to be about all this Caribbean stuff. I need new thrills, new challenges, and new experiences."

"Sir, I've been hoping for this for many years." Rodrigo let his hand slide down Christopher's back, coming to rest on his bum. "I love you, Christopher. I love you with all of my heart."

"Er, well, um, go and get some rum, Rod," whispered Columbus. "I can't do this sober."

Rodrigo sprinted to the ship, grabbed a bottle of his home brew, and sprinted back to find no sign of Christopher.

"Chris! Chris!" shouted Rodrigo.

"I'll be out in a minute," shouted Columbus from behind some sugarcane. "I'm dropping the kids off at the pool." And there he squatted for the next twenty minutes, contemplating life, wondering what would become of his New World. What would become of this Martinique place? Would it stay Spanish, or would the French snaffle it up like they did with Guadeloupe, the bastards?

"Right, Roddy boy," he said, proudly zipping up his trousers and letting out a relieved sigh. "Let's get pissed."

 SAINT LUCIA

OFFICIAL NAME: Saint Lucia
AREA: 617 sq km
POPULATION: 151,143 (2001 census)
CAPITAL: Castries
LANGUAGE(S): English

Saint Lucia is shaped like a teardrop. This is a man-made outline; the residents wanted to make some kind of gesture to show their grief after the death of Princess Diana.

 SAINT VINCENT and THE GRENADINES

OFFICIAL NAME: Saint Vincent and the Grenadines
AREA: 389 sq km
POPULATION: 111,821 (2001 est.)
CAPITAL: Kingstown
LANGUAGE(S): English

This sovereign island nation was named after the popular local mid-sixties beat group led by Arnold "The Saint" Vincent. Vincent's personal history could fill a book of its own. Born John Bassett and conjoined to his twin brother, James, John lived the first eighteen years of his life in Spalding, UK. While playing French cricket one day, the twins slipped and ripped apart. Sadly James passed on, but it was the break John needed. His marks at school got better, girls started touching his trousers, and his voice took on a wonderful timbre which led to him joining a local skiffle group, the Stingin' Rays. It was around this time he acquired his nickname, when he was spotted helping an old lady with her shopping. Rumours persist to this day that he was actually just trying to get his hands on her Twix. Not rumoured, though, were his charges of crimes against nature in the U.S. state of North Carolina. Frightened by the U.S. legal system, he fled to the Caribbean, grew a moustache, and changed his name to Arnold Vincent. Here he formed a group, got some backing singers from neighbouring Grenada, and christened them, first with his love seed, and then as the Grenadines. They played plenty of shows around Kingstown, and their island-hopping 1964 tour (taking in All Awash, Rabbit, Pigeon, Dove, and Cow & Calves Islands) was a great success, leading to their first number one hit "My Maybe Baby." Tragically, Vincent died in a car accident in 1976, and the nation mourned him with big, fat tears of salty water. Four years later, this previously untitled collection of islands was renamed in Arnold's honour.

 GRENADA

OFFICIAL NAME: Grenada
AREA: 344 sq km
POPULATION: 100,895 (2001 census)
CAPITAL: St. George's
LANGUAGE(S): English

In 1498, on his third visit to the New World, Christopher Columbus came across Grenada. His pal Rodrigo had been busy making eggnog in the galley, when he heard Chris summoning him to his hammock on the beach.

"Whazzzzzzzzzzup?" said Rodrigo. (This was back in the day when people still aped that Budweiser commercial.)

"Listen, Rod, much as I enjoy your eggnog, it's a bit...plain," he said, trying not to hurt Rodrigo's feelings. "How about putting some of this here nutmeg that I've just found on this here island in that there eggnog? Maybe it'll spice things up a bit and, who knows, it could act as some sort of laxative because I'm really backed up."

"I think that's a wonderful idea, my love. Er, I mean, sir," slipped Rod.

It was tasty, and Grenada went on to be the world's leading supplier of nutmeg until 1983 when Ronald Reagan decided that those nutmegs had the look of communists about them and sent some of his military in to fuck 'em up.

 BARBADOS

OFFICIAL NAME: Barbados
AREA: 430 sq km
POPULATION: 260,491 (1990 census)
CAPITAL: Bridgetown
LANGUAGE(S): English

Until 1966 all Barbadians had beards. Even the men. (Sorry.)

 TRINIDAD and TOBAGO

OFFICIAL NAME: Republic of Trinidad and Tobago
AREA: 5,128 sq km
POPULATION: 1,262,366 (2000 census)
CAPITAL: Port of Spain
LANGUAGE(S): English

Trinidad (the home of limbo dancing, steel drums, and calypso music) and Tobago (the home of, er, some trees) are so close they're virtually in South America; they're separated only by a thin channel of water called, scarily, the Serpent's Mouth. In fact, several people who decide which bit belongs in which continental area *do* think it's in South America. Not me, I think it's part of the Caribbean. Anyway, the relationship between Big Papa Trinidad and Baby Brother Tobago is such that the smaller of the two often feels worthless and shat upon. To combat this, armed guerrillas often swap the signs at the ferry terminals so that visitors think that Tobago is Trinidad and Trinidad is Tobago.

 ARUBA

OFFICIAL NAME: Aruba
AREA: 193 sq km
POPULATION: 90,506 (2000 census)
CAPITAL: Oranjestad
LANGUAGE(S): Dutch, Papiamento

Not far from Venezuela, Aruba is a self-governing part of the Netherlands. It was originally discovered by the Spanish but when the Dutch came along and wanted to arm wrestle for it, the Spanish let it go quite easily, because they'd built a big wall on the coast so that the Dutch couldn't see South America, which the Spanish were far more interested in.

The dry, arid climate of Aruba is important to the island's economy. The air is harvested and is the primary ingredient in most modern antiperspirants.

An Aruban arid air agricultural worker at harvest time.

SOUTH AMERICA

The southern bulk of the Americas looks a bit like an ice cream cone, and, ho ho, it's just as tasty! There's the Amazon and its rainforests, the Andes running down the western edge and, er, some other stuff…the odd lake here and there, but, y'know, we've all seen a lake, huh? Brave Europeans in the sixteenth century quickly battered the locals into submission and now most of the continent speaks Spanish and Portuguese. Take that, natives!

Mmm, vanilla! My favourite!

COLOMBIA

OFFICIAL NAME: República de Colombia (Republic of Colombia)
AREA: 1,141,568 sq km
POPULATION: 41,537,000 (1999 est.)
CAPITAL: Bogotá
LANGUAGE(S): Spanish

Famous for its cocaine production, wild-haired footballers, and all-round bad-assness, Columbia was, in the 1980s, the largest exporter of villains for *Miami Vice*. Since then, Colombia has created something of great beauty to take our minds off the nasty stuff: Shakira, a goddess among women who can shake it in a way that makes me strategically place a cushion in my lap.

VENEZUELA

OFFICIAL NAME: República Bolivariana de Venezuela (Bolivarian Republic of Venezuela)
AREA: 916,445 sq km
POPULATION: 23,054,210 (2001 census)
CAPITAL: Caracas
LANGUAGE(S): Spanish and thirty-one indigenous languages

Venezuela, an oil-rich nation on the northern coast of South America, was home to one of the continent's most favouritest sons, Simón Bolívar. He was the man who stood up and said, "Go back to Spain, you Spanish Spaniel Spaniards, we need you not!" He did that not only in Venezuela, but also in Bolivia, Colombia, Ecuador, Panama, and Peru. He also told some good blue jokes in the pub and always bought a round.[16]

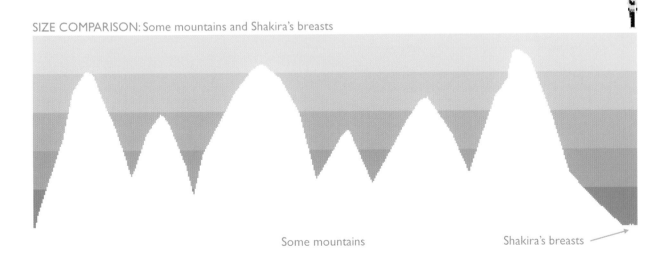

SIZE COMPARISON: Some mountains and Shakira's breasts

Some mountains   Shakira's breasts

GUYANA

OFFICIAL NAME: Co-operative Republic of Guyana
AREA: 215,083 sq km
POPULATION: 756,072 (1986 est.)
CAPITAL: Georgetown
LANGUAGE(S): English

Territorial disputes with Suriname and Venezuela on either side of Guyana—the home of Demerara sugar and the Jonestown Massacre—could, if the Guyanese were as cooperative as their official name would imply, make this already small nation nothing but a sliver of marshy plains and rainforests.

As it is, Guyana has plenty of mountains, and loads of dinosaurs. All kinds of adventures can be had here like jumping and swinging on vines and fighting apes and stuff. It's brill!

SURINAME

OFFICIAL NAME: Republiek Suriname (Republic of Suriname)
AREA: 163,820 sq km
POPULATION: 423,400 (1996 est.)
CAPITAL: Paramaribo
LANGUAGE(S): Dutch

In the mid-seventeeth century, the English and Dutch were having another big old battle about various stuff. When that all came to an end, and the opposing sides did the photo where they smile and pretend to sign a document, the Dutch traded Manhattan for Suriname. Like a secondhand car dealer swapping a clapped-out old banger for a Bentley, the English couldn't help but snigger.

"Hey, why all the laughter, guys?" asked van Gogh, the Dutch fella.

"Nothing! Honestly, just, y'know, a private joke about some bloke we know back in Ipswich," lied Peter, as he dug his elbow into his compatriot James to stop him from chuckling.

FRENCH GUIANA

OFFICIAL NAME: Guyane (Guiana)
AREA: 83,534 sq km
POPULATION: 191,000 (2005 est.)
CAPITAL: Cayenne
LANGUAGE(S): Go on, guess.

Not a proper country, just a bit of France that the French didn't like so much because it had a nasty prison on it. So they cut it off, attached a motor, and said, "Bon voyage!" Eventually this chunk of land, not known for its wines or cheeses or loose women, crashed into the northeast coast of Brazil, where it lives happily today like an abandoned puppy re-homed with a friendly new owner.

French Guiana motoring to its new home in South America.

ECUADOR

OFFICIAL NAME: República del Ecuador (Republic of Ecuador)
AREA: 272,045 sq km
POPULATION: 12,156,608 (2001 census)
CAPITAL: Quito
LANGUAGE(S): Spanish (Quechua and Shuar also official for the indigenous people)

Ecuador is the Spanish word for the equator, which, unsurprisingly, given the name, runs through the country. Ecuadorians come from miles around to look at the equator's imaginary glory. So proud of it are they that nobody is allowed to set foot on it. A series of tunnels and bridges were built in the 1960s to allow people to cross without touching its halfway-between-the-poles wonderfulness, a bit like how they build tunnels under roads so frogs don't die on their way to the river to spawn.

In 2009, Jean-Michel Jarre is planning a massive concert along the length of the Ecuadorian equator, with a laser harp erected one metre above the 0° latitude line, emitting a single, haunting New Age-y note (D minor). He will ride on a bicycle alongside the laser harp, rhythmically playing it with an oar.

 PERU

OFFICIAL NAME: República del Perú (Republic of Peru)
AREA: 1,285,216 sq km
POPULATION: 26,748,972 (2002 est.)
CAPITAL: Lima
LANGUAGE(S): Spanish, Quechua, Aymara

What is now Peru was once the centre of the Inca empire. They were getting along quite nicely, thank you very much, until the Spanish came along and laughed at them for worshiping a sun god (something they could see) rather than the Catholic God (something nobody's ever seen). Once they were done laughing, Diego y Pedro noticed there was a ton of gold just lying around, so they e-mailed their boss back in Madrid:

> Send more men. There's a crapload of gold here, and we can get really rich!
>
> There's some wicked funny animals that look like horse-goats; I'll send some photos in my next e-mail. Oh, and some of the chicks here are hot, too :)

Pretty pissed off with affairs as they were, the natives built a town on a mountain, made it look old and crumbly, and named it Machu Picchu (after the architect's pet bearded collies, Machu and Picchu) to attract middle-class European students and their parents' Western Union money.

Peru shares Lake Titicaca—the world's highest navigable lake—with its neighbour Bolivia. Like Timbuktu (in New Zealand) and Kathmandu (in Norway), Lake Titicaca is one of those places that everyone's heard of but doesn't know where it is. It probably isn't even where I've just said it is.

 BOLIVIA

OFFICIAL NAME: República de Bolivia (Republic of Bolivia)
AREA: 1,098,581 sq km
POPULATION: 8,274,325 (2001 census)
CAPITAL: La Paz (seat of government), Sucre (the legal capital)
LANGUAGE(S): Spanish, Aymara, Quechua

Bolivia's got two capitals. Fancy, huh?

It's also nicknamed the "Rooftop of the World," but that's mainly because there's a gutter running along the length of its borders.

 BRAZIL

OFFICIAL NAME: República Federativa do Brasil (Federative Republic of Brazil)
AREA: 8,514,047 sq km
POPULATION: 174,632,960 (2002 census)
CAPITAL: Brasília
LANGUAGE(S): Portuguese

The largest and most populous nation in South America, Brazil borders all the other South American countries but Ecuador and Chile.

Apart from the hill thingy with Jesus on the top, the beaches full of pubic-hairless beauties, that mountain made of sugar, the skillful kids playing football in the streets, millions of World Cup winners' medals, fancy carnivals, that lass from Ipanema, and that whopping great big river, there's plenty to know about Brazil. Like, er, y'know, umm, trains and food and, er, people and trees.

Those trees though are under threat from us all. Especially me, because the paper that this book is made from probably used to be a bit of Amazonian rainforest. An area the size of Brazil is being deforested every year. I blame the woodpeckers, though; Brazilian woodpeckers are the most destructive and antisocial of all birds.

Currently, the world of football is openmouthed with admiration for Brazilian player Ronaldinho. He's pretty good—not as good as me—but still pretty tasty. He can stand in the car park outside Barcelona's stadium, kick a ball in a southwest direction, go to the airport, get delayed because the flight was overbooked, have a few fajitas and a cappuccino while he waits, fly to Rio de Janeiro, spend ages going through immigration because he's mislaid his passport (he eventually finds it between the sick bag and the in-flight magazine back on the plane), get a cab to the beach, sign a few autographs, chat up a foxy lass with rather prominent nipples at one of those bars with the drinks in coconut shells, then saunter down to the water's edge and catch the ball on the back of his neck while playing level nine of *Tetris* on his Game Boy and wearing flip-flops made of fire.

Ronaldinho playing football in his flip-flops of fire.

 PARAGUAY

OFFICIAL NAME: República del Paraguay/Tetä Paraguáype (Republic of Paraguay)
AREA: 406,752 sq km
POPULATION: 5,206,101 (2002 est.)
CAPITAL: Asunción
LANGUAGE(S): Spanish, Guaraní

This landlocked nation is home to many of the world's finest parades and buildings with parabolic roofs. It's an exciting place with its paraplegics with paraphilia, parasailing paratroopers with parasols, paranoiacs paraphrasing parables, paramilitaries sending parakeets to paramours in Paraguarí, paramedics prescribing Paracetamol, poets composing pararhymes (and finishing them off with fancy paraphs), and Paralympians parachuting onto parapets. That's the end of this paragraph about Paraguay, a nation full of paragons of parallel parking.

 URUGUAY

OFFICIAL NAME: República Oriental del Uruguay (Oriental Republic of Uruguay)
AREA: 176,215 sq km
POPULATION: 3,360,868 (2002 est.)
CAPITAL: Montevideo
LANGUAGE(S): Spanish

Snuggled between Argentina and Brazil, Uruguay's capital is soon to be renamed Montedvd to make it sound less eighties.

 ARGENTINA

OFFICIAL NAME: República Argentina (Argentine Republic)
AREA: 2,780,092 sq km
POPULATION: 36,223,947 (2001 census)
CAPITAL: Buenos Aries
LANGUAGE(S): Spanish

Argentina is the second largest country in South America and is named after the fictional country in a song from Andrew Lloyd Webber's musical, *Starlight Express*. Only jokin'!

Actually, it was named by the indigenous Diaguita folk. Knowing how much the Spaniards liked shiny metal, they borrowed the Latin word for silver, *argentum*, and made it a bit more Spanishy by lopping of the -um and adding -ina. This was all done in an effort to boost tourism, especially when combined with the rumours they started of mountains being made of pure silver.

It did more than simply boost tourism, though. It brought so many holiday makers that they took over. Liking the Diaguitas' style, top politician Manuel Belgrano decided to make the flag of Argentina really pretty to attract more people. He picked a nice blue and stuck a white stripe in the middle. Feeling a bit chipper that day, he drew a smiley sun in the middle. That really did the trick and loads more people moved to Argentina after seeing the sunny flag.

Legend has it that the Patagonia area of Argentina is populated by giants. Only the Welsh were brave enough to move to that region because they love a good giant. Seeing how tales of scary giants were buggering up tourism, Argentina decided to invent a really little fellow to be the most famous Argentine[17] ever, Diego Maradona.

Eva Perón; Ernesto "Che" Guevara; transvestite actress Florencia De La V; liberator of Argentina José de San Martín; tennis dish Gabriela Sabatini; and some footballers: Real Madrid legend Alfredo Di Stéfano, Gabriel Batistuta, Osvaldo Ardiles, and the best footballer ever, Diego Armando Maradona.

CHILE

OFFICIAL NAME: República de Chile (Republic of Chile)
AREA: 756,096 sq km
POPULATION: 15,116,435 (2002 census)
CAPITAL: Santiago
LANGUAGE(S): Spanish

When carving up South America, the Europeans thought it'd be a right laugh to make a funny-shaped country. Thus Chile is dead long and thin. The Spanish, though, had quite a fight on their hands when they wanted to grab the land because the native Mapuche chaps were a bit tasty with their fists and knew karate.

After a few hundred years of chuckling at the shape of their own country and building the Andes to attract mountaineers, Chileans looked out the window and found themselves under the dictatorship of General Augusto Pinochet. He was a pal of Margaret Thatcher, the former British prime minister, and an utter cunt.[18] These two facts are connected.

FALKLAND ISLANDS

OFFICIAL NAME: Falkland Islands
AREA: 12,173 sq km
POPULATION: 2,967 (2005 est.)
CAPITAL: Stanley
LANGUAGE(S): English, goddamn it

From a 1982 pamphlet issued by the UK Ministry of Defence titled *Daddy's Coming Home Soon—Explaining the Falklands War to Your Child*:

> Jimmy had a toy bear. Although he liked the bear, he'd forgotten all about it and had stuffed it in the back of the closet under the stairs.
>
> One day, his sister Jane found the bear and began playing with it. When Jimmy saw Jane playing with the bear, he got upset and torpedoed her Barbie doll collection to smithereens.
>
> "That'll fucking teach her to mess with my shit," said Jimmy.

Anyway, the Falkland Islands belong to the UK. Argentina wants the islands too but, being foreign, they have a weird name for them: Islas Malvinas.

There are lots of sheep and penguins here. They like nothing better than to nip down to the cybercafé to play *Battleship* online.

Sixteenth-century map of South America.

A sheep.

North
America

Labrador
Sea

Denmark Strait

ROCKALL

U.K.

Bay of
Biscay

Europe

Titanic
X

AZORES

ATLANTIC
OCEAN

BERMUDA

MADEIRA

CANARY
ISLANDS

Gulf of
Mexico

CAPE
VERDE

Africa

Caribbean Sea

Sierra
Leone Basin

Gulf of Guinea

SÃO
TOMÉ
& PRINCIPE

SAINT PETER &
SAINT PAUL ROCKS

South
America

ASCENSION
ISLAND

Angola
Basin

St. HELENA

A MAP OF THE ATLANTIC OCEAN

SCALE   1: 3.14159265358979323846 26

EVERESTS

0   1

0   1

QOMOLANGMAS

MARTIN
VAZ

TRINDADE

TRISTAN
DA CUNHA

Cape
Basin

Argentine
Basin

Gulf of San Matías

Gulf of San Jorge

Falkland Islands

SOUTH
GEORGIA

BOUVET ISLAND

SOUTH
SANDWICH
ISLANDS

SOUTHERN OCEAN

Weddell
Sea

Antarctica

ATLANTIC OCEAN

It's the planet's second biggest ocean, and if it was cola, it'd fill about 1,078,666,670,000,000 cans. The Atlantic is bounded by the Americas on one side, Europe and Asia on the other, and the Arctic and Southern Oceans at the poles. Exactly where those last two borders are is anybody's guess.

It gets quite deep in the Atlantic, so you can't really roll your jeans up and paddle out very far. You wouldn't want to, really, because it'd get a bit cold and you'd probably not get back in time for dinner.

One of the best bits of the Atlantic is the Gulf Stream, a warm and fast current that helps bring nice-ish weather to the British Isles. It's not without its problems, though. The fish in the colder bits of the Atlantic get jealous and try to sneak into the Gulf Stream. The porous borders mean sharks and dolphins are always darting in and eating all the krill, bringing their whole families along, and not bothering to learn the Gulf Stream fish slang.

Due to the number of ships that have crossed the Atlantic, lots of pirates have invented shanties about her waters. This one is typical of the late nineteenth century, usually sung in a call-and-response style with the captain bellowing the first line and his crew replying with something about fish.

> The Atlantic waters drench us,
> But we love to eat her fish.
> There's deep Atlantic trenches,
> Full! Oh full o' fish.
> We like to eat the tenches,
> But they're freshwater fish.
> We fondle mermaid wenches
> Cos they're fish with tits.

Anyway, enough of the fish stuff. There are several bits of land plonked into the Atlantic Ocean.

AZORES

OFFICIAL NAME: Região Autónoma dos Açores (Autonomous Region of the Azores)
AREA: 2,333 sq km
POPULATION: 241,763 (2001 est.)
CAPITAL: Three of 'em—Ponta Delgado, Angra do Heroísmo, and Horta
LANGUAGE(S): Portuguese

Lots of chores in the Azores occur outdoors. It's sunny, see.

If I was the manager of the Corrs or the Doors I'd have had them do live albums in the Azores.

MADEIRA

OFFICIAL NAME: Região Autónoma da Madeira (Autonomous Region of Madeira)
AREA: 797 sq km
POPULATION: 250,000 (1991 est.)
CAPITAL: Funchal
LANGUAGE(S): Portuguese

One big, floaty—and slightly soggy—lemon-flavoured cake.

CANARY ISLANDS

OFFICIAL NAME: Comunidad Autónoma de Canarias (Autonomous Community of the Canaries)
AREA: 7,447 sq km
POPULATION: 1,968,280 (2005 est.)
CAPITAL: Las Palmas de Gran Canaria and Santa Cruz de Tenerife
LANGUAGE(S): Spanish

This Spanish territory's national dish is fish and chips. The traditional way to order this delicacy is loud and slow and full of xenophobic bile: Fish. Fiiiiiiiish! FISH! (mime fish swimming with hand) a-a-a-n-n-d chips. C-h-i-p-s. Chips. And a pint—a piiiiinnnt—of lager. Laaaaarrgah! What? Don't you understand English? Bloody foreigners....

CAPE VERDE

OFFICIAL NAME: República de Cabo Verde (Republic of Cape Verde)
AREA: 4,033 sq km
POPULATION: 434,812 (2000 census)
CAPITAL: Praia
LANGUAGE(S): Portuguese

Originally set up as a big slavery supermarket where Portuguese folk could come and pick up great slaves at low, low prices: three Senegalese slaves for the price of two; two years, no money down; 0 percent interest on bulk orders of Guineans; and be sure to check out the astounding bargains that can be found in our pre-owned slave department. With prices like that you'd be crazy to produce sugarcane yourself!

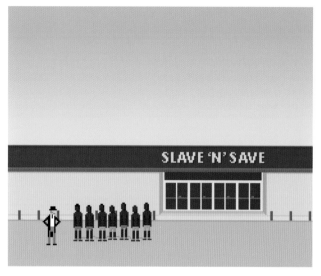

Seven happy Africans with their new European pal.

SAINT PETER and PAUL ROCKS

OFFICIAL NAME: Penedos de São Pedro e São Paulo
AREA: 10 sq km
POPULATION: some crabs
CAPITAL: Zico
LANGUAGE(S): Portuguese

Twelve little volcanic islands located between the bumpy bits of Africa and Brazil. Charles Darwin stopped here to take a piss once. Nowadays it's where the Brazilians dump all the waxed-off pubic hair.

ASCENSION ISLAND

OFFICIAL NAME: Ascension Island
AREA: 35 sq km
POPULATION: 1,100 (2005 est.)
CAPITAL: Georgetown
LANGUAGE(S): English

A petrol station built on a rock so the Brits could fill their tanks and get a Cornish pasty on their way to the Falklands.

SAINT HELENA

OFFICIAL NAME: Saint Helena
AREA: 410 sq km
POPULATION: 4,918 (2005 est.)
CAPITAL: Jamestown
LANGUAGE(S): English

An overseas territory of the UK, and most famous for being where Napoleon Bonaparte was exiled to in 1815. He spent much of his time dictating his memoirs in really boring detail. Like this:

> 22 June, 1812 was a good day. I woke up and had a cup of coffee. Then I did a wee. Then I did a poo and read the *Paris Business Review*. My stocks were up, so I was happy. Then I brushed my teeth. Then I looked out of the window and saw Madame Jolie in her bloomers across the street. I think she knows I'm watching. Then I knocked over a vase and the water went on the rug and I had to clean it up. Then I went downstairs and brushed my hair. Then I went outside and got on my horse and invaded Russia.

TRINDADE and MARTIM VAZ

OFFICIAL NAME: Derek
AREA: 10.4 sq km
POPULATION: 32 military dudes
CAPITAL: Pelé
LANGUAGE(S): Portuguese

Nothing more than a couple of rocks in the ocean that the Brazilian army uses to practice its football skills. With cannonballs.

TRISTAN DA CUNHA

OFFICIAL NAME: Tristan da Cunha
AREA: 201 sq km
POPULATION: 273 (2006 census)
CAPITAL: Edinburgh of the Seven Seas
LANGUAGE(S): English

A dependency of the British overseas territory of Saint Helena, Tristan da Cuhna is a bunch of six islands and a smattering of rocks nearly halfway between Cape Town and Montevideo. Apart from a spot of fishing, the main source of income is selling stamps to nerds around the world. This tends to bring in, ooooh, about thirty-two pence every day or so.

All but one of the islands are wheelchair accessible. Helpfully, the one without a ramp is called Inaccessible Island.

Inaccessible Island's wheelchair-unfriendly dock and stepping-stones arrangement.

BOUVET ISLAND

OFFICIAL NAME: Bouvetøya
AREA: 49 sq km
POPULATION: 0 (2004)
CAPITAL: You're kidding, right?
LANGUAGE(S): Er, seal?

No discos here, party animals. Only some glaciers and, er, that's it. Bouvet Island is about as remote as you can get, plopped about halfway between South Africa and Antarctica. It was discovered by some French bloke called Bouvet. He quickly buggered off home. A couple of Brits had a poke around, just having a look to see if the French guy had left any porn behind, but it wasn't until 1927 when some plucky Norwegians turned up that anyone properly bothered to claim the land. That was because they *did* find a couple of saucy French postcards hidden under a rock and figured Bouvet Island might well be the porn volcano that the Vikings had talked about.

SOUTH GEORGIA and SOUTH SANDWICH ISLANDS

OFFICIAL NAME: South Georgia and South Sandwich Islands
AREA: 3,093 sq km
POPULATION: about 20 scientists
CAPITAL: Grytviken
LANGUAGE(S): English

A bunch of rocks in the middle of nowhere, way east of the Falkland Islands.

Discovered by Captain James Cook back in the day, South Georgia was named after some lass he fancied, and the South Sandwich Islands were named after a cheese-and-pickle sandwich he, after many months at sea without much in the way of good snacks, regrets not having eaten before his voyage because, he said, he'd "pick something up from the McDonald's Sail-Thru." There was no McDonald's.

It's virtually all glaciers and stuff down here, so nothing much happens. There's nothing but some penguins and a gaggle of scientists doing sciencey stuff, singing "God Save The Queen," and watching the same porn videos over and over again.

. . .

Other lumps in the Atlantic Ocean covered in other chapters include Iceland, Ireland, Faroe Islands, the United Kingdom, Greenland, Saint-Pierre and Miquelon, Bermuda, the various bits belonging to the United States and Canada, the Falkland Islands, and São Tomé and Príncipe.

A MAP of AFRICA

SCALE 1:76 000 000
CUBITS
0 — 1 — 2 — 3 — 4
0 — 2 — 4 — 6 — 8
VIRGATES

Plazas de Soberanía
SPAIN
ALGIERS
BIT OF ITALY
TUNIS
CRETE
CYPRUS
Mediterranean Sea
RABAT
Casablanca
MOROCCO
Atlas Mountains
Sfax
TRIPOLI
DOUBLECI
Alexandria
CAIRO
Arabian Peninsula
LAÂYOUNE
WESTERN SAHARA
ALGERIA
LIBYA
EGYPT
Luxor
Nile
RED SEA
MAURITANIA
NOVAKCHOTT
S a h a r a
MALI
NIGER
CHAD
DARFUR
KHARTOUM
SUDAN
ERITREA
DAKAR
SENEGAL
GAMBIA
BISSAU
GUINEA BISSAU
BAMAKO
BURKINA FASO
NIAMEY
Lake Chad
NDJAMENA
DJIBOUTI
Gulf of Aden
SOM...
CONAKRY
FREETOWN
GUINEA
OUAGADOUGOU
NIGERIA
ABUJA
CENTRAL AFRICAN REPUBLIC
(Nile goes on forever)
ETHIOPIA
ADDIS ABABA
MONROVIA
SIERRA LEONE
(sorry, I fucked up.
This is really LIBERIA)
CÔTE D'IVOIRE
GHANA
TOGO
BENIN
LAGOS
ABIDJAN
ACCRA
PORTO-NOVO
LOME
CAMEROON
BANGUI
YAOUNDÉ
EQ. GUINEA
SÃO TOMÉ & PRINCIPE
LIBREVILLE
CONGO
GABON
Congo Basin
DEM. REP CONGO
RWANDA
KIGALI
UGANDA
KAMPALA
KENYA
Lake Turkana
NAIROBI
Lake Victoria
MOGADISHU
SOMALIA
ATLANTIC OCEAN
BRAZZAVILLE
KINSHASA
A little bit of Angola
BUJUMBURA
BURUNDI
Lake Tanganyika
TANZANIA
Mombasa
ZANZIBAR
DARES SALAAM
SEYCHELLES
LUANDA
ANGOLA
Lilongwe
MALAWI
COMOROS
MAYOTTE
ZAMBIA
LUSAKA
HARARE
ZIMBABWE
MOZAMBIQUE
MADAGASCAR
ANTANANARIVO
MAURITI...
RÉUNION
NAMIBIA
BOTSWANA
Kalahari Desert
WINDHOEK
GABORONE
JOHANNESBURG
Pretoria
MBABANE
MAPUTO
Soweto
SWAZILAND
INDIAN OCEAN
SOUTH AFRICA
MASERU
LESOTHO
Cape Town

AFRICA

Africa looks like one of those frozen processed lamb steaklettes that were pretty popular in my family's kitchen in the mid-eighties. Africa is where human beings come from. It's where we evolved from chimps and monkeys and became the people we are today.

The Europeans and Americans repaid the Africans for creating the species by first stealing their people and forcing them to do some farming, then by nicking their land and forcing them to do more farming. What nice folks those Europeans and Americans are.

Of course, these days, Africa is most famous for its hungry kids, life-threatening diseases, and the occasional power-crazed leader riding around in a big 1970s olive-green Mercedes Benz.

North Africa

WESTERN SAHARA

OFFICIAL NAME: Al-Sahra' al-Garbiyah (Western Sahara)
AREA: 266,000 sq km
POPULATION: 341,000 (2005 est.)
CAPITAL: none (largest city is El Aaiún)
LANGUAGE(S): Arabic

Western Sahara isn't a proper country, but a Non-Self-Governing Territory next to the Atlantic Ocean. Spain used to be the boss here but the Spaniards got a bit bored of making sandcastles so they went home and told the Moroccans and Mauritanians that they could divvy it up how they wanted. It's still not sorted though because, understandably, the folks living here fancy all the sand for themselves, thank you very much.

He can build four million of these should he feel like it, the lucky fellow!

MOROCCO

OFFICIAL NAME: Al-Mamlakah al-Maghribiyah (Kingdom of Morocco)
AREA: 710,850 sq km
POPULATION: 29,891,708 (2004 census)
CAPITAL: Rabat
LANGUAGE(S): Arabic

The lowlands and low plateaus that are near the Atlantic Ocean are the richest and most populous bits of Morocco but most of the country's landscape is dominated by the Atlas Mountains. A small insurgency of mountains called the Anti-Atlas range operates within the southwest of the Atlas Mountains. The main objective of the Anti-Atlas forces is the establishment of some snow on their peaks so they can get some skiing action going on.

PLAZAS DE SOBERANÍA

OFFICIAL NAME: Plazas de Soberanía (Places of Sovereignty)
AREA: 48-ish sq km
POPULATION: 145,000 (2005 est.)
CAPITAL: none
LANGUAGE(S): Spanish

The Plazas de Soberanía are five separate places on the northern coast of Morocco. They are possessions of Spain. The two big places are Ceuta and Melilla. That's where most people live. The three smaller places are called Islas Chafarinas, Peñón de Alhucemas, and Peñón de Vélez de la Gomera. Morocco would like these tiny places back. Spain wants to keep them. Sorry, but I couldn't give a shit either way.

ALGERIA

OFFICIAL NAME: Al-Jumhuriyah al-Jaza'iriyah ad-Dimuqratiyah ash-Sha'biyah (People's Democratic Republic of Algeria)
AREA: 2,381,741 sq km
POPULATION: 29,273,343 (1998 census)
CAPITAL: Algiers
LANGUAGE(S): Arabic

Run by France for a long time, Algeria gained independence in 1954 when the Algerian National Liberation Front kicked their Gallic asses all the way back across the Mediterranean. Sadly for the Algerians, though, they didn't notice Zinedine Zidane's parents also going across the sea to Marseille, depriving them of one of the best football players in the world.[19]

TUNISIA

OFFICIAL NAME: Al-Jumhuriyah at-Tunisiyah (Republic of Tunisia)
AREA: 163,610 sq km
POPULATION: 9,910,872 (2004 census)
CAPITAL: Tunis
LANGUAGE(S): Arabic

Tunisia's queen is the well-known pop singer Dido. "White Flag" is still number one in the Tunisian charts, and any record that approaches selling more copies in any given week is promptly banned. Most people secretly want to shoot themselves every time it comes on the radio.[20]

LIBYA

OFFICIAL NAME: Al-Jamahiriyah al-'Arabiyah al-Libiyah ash Sha'biyah al-Ishtirakiyah al-'Uzma (Great Socialist People's Libyan Arab Jamahiriya)
AREA: 1,759,540 sq km
POPULATION: 4,811,902 (1995 census)
CAPITAL: Tripoli
LANGUAGE(S): Arabic

I can safely say that there's never gonna be a day when I will remember Libya's full official Arabic name. But I will always remember their flag, being, as it is, just a field of green. I can't decide whether this is the best flag in the world or the worst flag in the world. Apparently, though, it looks like that because Colonel Gaddafi—Libya's "Guide of the First of September Great Revolution of the Socialist People's Libyan Arab Jamahiriya" or, for brevity's sake, "leader"—is a massive snooker fan and putting a whole snooker table at the top of a flagpole was a bit too much hassle.

EGYPT

OFFICIAL NAME: Jumhuriah Misr al-'Arabiyah (Arab Republic of Egypt)
AREA: 997,739 sq km
POPULATION: 70,548,713 (2004 est. Actually, I'm not sure how it is that they can be so precise in their estimations; surely an estimate is when you say, "Pfff, I guess it's about seventy and a half million people"?)
CAPITAL: Cairo
LANGUAGE(S): Arabic

Egypt is an independent nation at the centre of the Arab region with a rather splendid history. While northern Europeans were still busy grunting at their oxen in the hope that they'd lay some eggs, the Egyptians were getting on with being dead clever by inventing board games and paper and those male and female signs on toilet doors. They also liked cats. That was their downfall, really. The Persians came along one day, showed them some pictures of *their* cats to distract them, then let the Rottweilers loose while they were still ooh-ing and aah-ing. While the Pharoahs sobbed uncontrollably, the Persians took over and started digging the Suez Canal. Once that was done, the Brits rolled in, said, "Thank you very much, this is ours now, you silly foreigners," and sat on the banks of the Nile sipping tea and complaining about the heat.

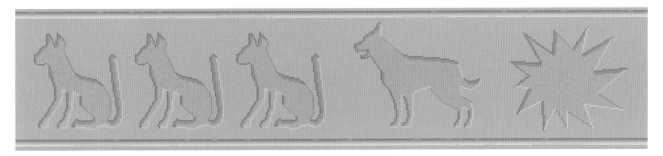

An ancient Egyptian newspaper's report of the Rottweiler attack.

Since then there's been the odd barney with Israel, a song by the Bangles, and lots of tourists wondering where the nose went.

 SUDAN

OFFICIAL NAME: Jumhuriyat as-Sudan (Republic of Sudan)
AREA: 2,503,890 sq km
POPULATION: 30,349,304 (2000 est.)
CAPITAL: Khartoum (executive), Omdurman (legislative)
LANGUAGE(S): Arabic, English

In the sixteenth century, Sudan was ruled by some people called the Funj. They were so much fun they had a J at the end of their name just for a laugh. It was all bouncy castles, mini golf, and clowns with squirty flowers back then. Until, that is, the Egyptians came along with their moody cats and stuff, and turned everything into a right bummer.

But help was at hand, in the form of those jolly Brits who were snaffling up as much of the world as possible in an effort to get some people to play cricket with them. Wishing to impart some of his military and colonial knowledge onto the "savages," a Britisher called Peter took a young native aside.

"Listen here, old bean," said Peter, whittling an ivory tusk into an oboe for his wife. "What we're going to do is create two colonies, one in the north and one in the south of this God-forsaken sandpit you call home. And here's some advice should the King's Empire ever fall, which I bloody well doubt, but anyway: Number one, tuck your shirt in and put some shoes on! You're not at a bloody holiday camp, man. Number two, keep this north-south divide going. By Jove! It's a winning policy!"

And with that, Peter beat the young chap to within an inch of his life and went off to eat some puréed giraffe's wings.

So, by the time Sudan gained independence in 1956, the north and south were already at it, hammer and tongs. This went on until 1972, when they decided to have a break and went about their own business for eleven years until President Gaafar Nimeiry fancied having the south as well as the north. Twenty years and over two million dead Sudanese later, some sort of agreement was come to where, again, the south is kinda in control of its own affairs.

But the happy days didn't last too long. Feeling a bit peeved about being in a neglected part of the country, some rebels in Darfur started demanding the good stuff. More fighting, loads of dead people, words like "ethnic cleansing" and "genocide"... It's all gone tits-up, and is anything but funj.

West Africa

MAURITANIA

OFFICIAL NAME: Al-Jumhuriyah al-Islamiyah al-Muritaniyah
(Islamic Republic of Mauritania)
AREA: 1,030,700 sq km
POPULATION: 2,508,159 (2000 census)
CAPITAL: Nouakchott
LANGUAGE(S): Arabic

The only country in the world with its borders drawn
with an Etch A Sketch.

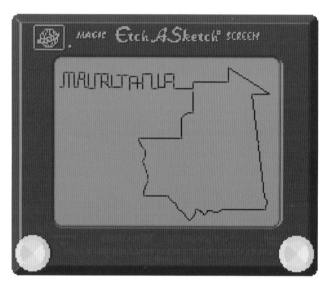

The government's original work of the borders of their nation.

SENEGAL

OFFICIAL NAME: République du Sénégal (Republic of Senegal)
AREA: 196,722 sq km
POPULATION: 9,967,215 (2002 census)
CAPITAL: Dakar
LANGUAGE(S): French

Senegal's capital, Dakar, is, as I'm sure you are aware, the
destination point of the participants of the Dakar Rally.
Although the origins of this very long race are unclear,
it is thought that the rally's original contestants had no
destination in mind and just kept going 'til they, er, fell
in the ocean. Since then, they've brought the finish line
forward a few hundred feet.

THE GAMBIA

OFFICIAL NAME: Republic of The Gambia
AREA: 10,689 sq km
POPULATION: 1,364,507 (2003 census)
CAPITAL: Banjul
LANGUAGE(S): English

Shaped like a tongue performing cunnilingus on Senegal,
The Gambia's borders were worked out by using the
fattest marker pen possible and drawing along the banks
of the Gambia River on a map. They grow peanuts there.
Loads of them. Anyone with a nut allergy should probably
not bother coming here on holiday.

MALI

OFFICIAL NAME: République du Mali (Republic of Mali)
AREA: 1,248,574 sq km
POPULATION: 10,179,170 (1998 census)
CAPITAL: Bamako
LANGUAGE(S): French

"Oh yeah?" said Mali, looking at a map of Mauritania.
"We did it too, *and* we did it last week; we were first, so
there!"

GUINEA-BISSAU

OFFICIAL NAME: Républica da Guiné-Bissau (Republic of Guinea-
Bissau)
AREA: 36,125 sq km
POPULATION: 1,295,841 (2004 est.)
CAPITAL: Bissau
LANGUAGE(S): Portuguese

For such a small country Guinea-Bissau has lots of super
wildlife goin' on, from its coastal swamps to its interior
forests and northern savannah. Pelicans, crocodiles,
snakes, apes, parrots, hyenas, crocodiles, leopards, and
flamingos all wish the humans would just fuck off with
that civil war shit.

GUINEA

OFFICIAL NAME: République de Guinée (Republic of Guinea)
AREA: 245,836 sq km
POPULATION: 7,156,406 (1996 census)
CAPITAL: Conakry
LANGUAGE(S): French

Guinea proclaimed itself independent from French rule in 1958. The French folk in Conakry, feeling rather miffed, blew a collective raspberry at the locals as they got in their Citroëns, and took their Johnny Halliday records and long, thin baking trays home to Paris. The subsequent baguette shortage created havoc and unrest, leaving president Ahmed Sekou Toure with no option but to torture and execute thousands of his countrymen.

SIERRA LEONE

OFFICIAL NAME: Republic of Sierra Leone
AREA: 71,740 sq km
POPULATION: 4,963,298 (2004 census)
CAPITAL: Freetown
LANGUAGE(S): English

When Sierra Leoneans see pictures of the rich and famous at obscenely decadent parties, wearing expensive frocks and jewellery, I wonder if they think, a) "ooh look, my son probably did the mining that resulted in that lovely diamond bracelet," or b) "ooh look, the bracelet stays around her wrist perfectly because she's not had her hand amputated like I have by the rebels who were funded by the mining of the aforementioned diamonds."

LIBERIA

OFFICIAL NAME: Republic of Liberia
AREA: 99,067 sq km
POPULATION: 1,826,143 (1999 est.)
CAPITAL: Monrovia
LANGUAGE(S): English

Liberia is Africa's oldest republic. Founded by freed American and Caribbean slaves, Liberia managed to keep the sticky fingers of Britain and France out. Nowadays, Liberia is one of the world's biggest producers of rubber, something that led children's TV art show, *Art Attack,* to choose Liberia as the location for its largest "Big Art Attack": a massive picture of a pygmy hippopotamus made from car tyres.

The Art Attack *hippo.*

CÔTE D'IVOIRE

OFFICIAL NAME: République de Côte d'Ivoire (Republic of Côte d'Ivoire)
AREA: 320,803 sq km
POPULATION: 17,065,000 (2002 est.)
CAPITAL: Abidjan (de facto)
LANGUAGE(S): French

The problem with having an ivory coast is that it really isn't much fun sunbathing and reading your Patricia Cornwell next to a big pile of rotting elephant carcasses.

An elephant dreams how different things could've been had evolution taken a few different turns.

BURKINA FASO

OFFICIAL NAME: Burkina Faso
AREA: 267,950 sq km
POPULATION: 10,373,341 (1996 census)
CAPITAL: Ouagadougou
LANGUAGE(S): French

Burkina Faso means "Land of Honest Men." This is useful when asking for the time, enquiring if there's a public lavatory nearby, or if you've not got a mirror handy and think you might have spinach between your teeth.

GHANA

OFFICIAL NAME: Republic of Ghana
AREA: 238,533 sq km
POPULATION: 18,845,265 (2000 census)
CAPITAL: Accra
LANGUAGE(S): English

Ghanaians were so happy when Spandau Ballet decided to shoot a pop video for "Gold" on one of their beaches that they renamed the nation Gold Coast after the song in question. Ghanaians were so distraught after the band's split that they re-renamed their nation.

TOGO

OFFICIAL NAME: République Togolaise (Togolese Republic)
AREA: 56,785 sq km
POPULATION: 5,227,227 (2005 est.)
CAPITAL: Lomé
LANGUAGE(S): French

Like a milk tooth, if you wiggled it Togo might fall out.

BENIN

OFFICIAL NAME: République du Bénin (Republic of Benin)
AREA: 112,622 sq km
POPULATION: 6,769,914 (2002 census)
CAPITAL: Porto-Novo
LANGUAGE(S): French

Benin was once the centre of the old African kingdom of Dahomey. Noticing that their neighbours Ivory Coast and Gold Coast (now Ghana) had "coast" in their names, preceded by something that fancy Europeans liked owning, the rulers of Dahomey got to thinking, "What could our coast be?"

Someone suggested that they sell ice cream and Fanta, someone else suggested having a rollercoaster, but they plumped for being the Slave Coast and selling slaves—plentiful supplies of which were gathered from inland villages—to the Dutch and Portuguese.

Nowadays though, Benin is one of Africa's most stable nations, and once a year followers of voodoo gather at the "point of no return" on the beach where slave ships once set sail and celebrate National Voodoo Day, which looks like a lot of fun.

NIGER

OFFICIAL NAME: République du Niger (Republic of Niger)
AREA: 1,189,546 sq km
POPULATION: 10,790,352 (2001 census)
CAPITAL: Naimey
LANGUAGE(S): French

Not the sort of country where you want a sticky *G* on your computer's keyboard.

NIGERIA

OFFICIAL NAME: Federal Republic of Nigeria
AREA: 923,768 sq km
POPULATION: 98,967,768 (1995 est.)
CAPITAL: Abuja
LANGUAGE(S): English

So, I got this e-mail from a guy in Nigeria saying that if I can give him a hand getting some money out of the country, I'd get 10 percent of it. Sounded like a good deal to me.

Haven't heard from him in a while. He's probably just busy, I guess.

Football players Jay-Jay Okocha and Nwankwo Kano; music guy Fela Kuti; music lass Sade; president Olusegun Obasanjo; writer, poet, and playwright Wole Soyinka; environmental activist Ken Saro-Wiwa; and Miss World 2001, Agbani Darego.

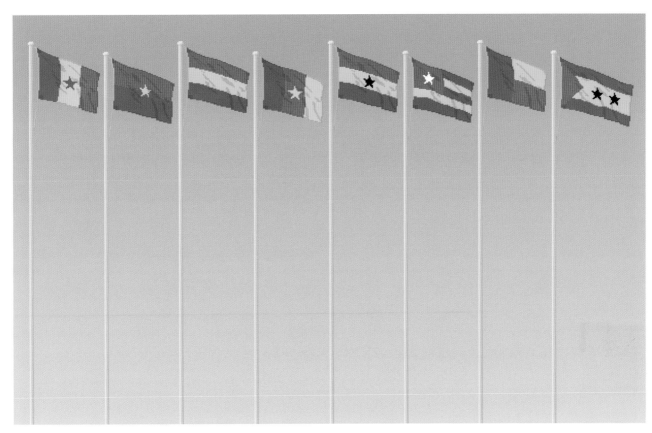

West African Flag Quiz

Lots of flags of West African nations look very similar. They were probably all done at one of those machines in the train station. This machine seems to only have a few templates and not very many colours. Can you guess which is which?

Middle Africa

 CHAD

OFFICIAL NAME: Jumhuriyah Tschad/République du Tschad (Republic of Chad)
AREA: 1,284,000 sq km
POPULATION: 6,279,931 (1993 census)
CAPITAL: N'Djamena
LANGUAGE(S): Arabic, French

The chunk of land that is now known as Chad was once a chunk of land with lots of different tribes. As they were going around snapping up countries to be part of their colonial system, two Frenchy fellows—emboldened by a victorious punch-up in Cameroon—had a swim in Lake Chad. "This is bon and très refreshing," said Pierre, splashing his arms around in the water.

"Oui, Pierre," his pal Jacques concurred.

"Oui, it's brilliant. Magnifique, even!" said Pierre, still thrashing around, but now spluttering his words between gulps of water.

"Mon ami, are you okay there?" said Jacques. "You look like you're having a little bit of trouble."

Jacques quickly rescued Pierre and swam him to the shore.

"Well, that was wonderful. Oh, and thanks for, y'know, saving me and stuff," said Pierre as he dusted the wet sand out from between his toes. "Let me just pop my socks and shoes on, and we can go and have another fight with that Sudanese warlord homme over on the other side of the lake."

With their laces tied and hair still a bit wet, Pierre et Jacques clattered into Rabih az-Zubayr, the Sudanese warlord, and head-butted him in the chest until death's cloak shrouded him.

"Superbe!" shouted Pierre, as he lit a cigarette and flung a string of onions around his neck for dramatic effect. "I wonder what we can do tomorrow...."

A Central African child's drawing of Pierre.

CENTRAL AFRICAN REPUBLIC

OFFICIAL NAME: République Centrafricaine (Central African Republic)
AREA: 622,436 sq km
POPULATION: 2,688,426 (1988 census)
CAPITAL: Bangui
LANGUAGE(S): French, Sango

Having a morning stroll the day after they'd snagged Chad, two French colonialists named Pierre et Jacques chanced upon a bit of land between the Ubangi and Shari rivers. Pierre stroked his waxy moustache and tried to look clever. "Have you got a headache?" asked Jacques, rummaging around his satchel looking for the ibuprofen. "Non, Jacques, non!" replied Pierre, "I think this is a new country I've found here. I will call it...erm..."

Pierre looked in pain again.

"What, Pierre, what will you call it?" whispered Jacques. Pierre's mind had gone blank. Jacques looked at the map then tentatively suggested, "Maybe c'est la République Centrafricaine!" Pierre sniggered. "That's a rubbish name," he thought.

On returning to Paris, everyone else agreed and decided to call it the Ubangi-Shari.

Jacques had the last laugh, though; upon achieving independence, the Central Africans decided that République Centrafricaine was in fact a pretty good name after all, and all the children did drawings of Pierre looking stupid, holding up a sign saying, "Ooh la la, I am stupid Pierre!"

CAMEROON

OFFICIAL NAME: République du Cameroun/Republic of Cameroon
AREA: 475,442 sq km
POPULATION: 15,731,000 (2001 est.)
CAPITAL: Yaoundé
LANGUAGE(S): French, English

My mum used to make coconut cameroons when I was a kid. They were really tasty.

EQUATORIAL GUINEA

OFFICIAL NAME: República de Guinea Ecuatorial/République du Guinée Équatoriale
AREA: 28,051 sq km
POPULATION: 406,200 (1994 census)
CAPITAL: Malabo
LANGUAGE(S): Spanish, French

Since gaining independence from Spain in 1968, Equatorial Guinea has had two leaders. Francisco Macías Nguema was the first. He ruled until 1979 when his nephew Teodoro Obiang Nguema Mbasogo staged a coup d'état after he failed to receive the toys he requested for his birthday. He then executed his uncle and has spent the years since then pocketing the money from oil production and torturing anyone who doesn't agree with what he says. What a nice fellow.

SÃO TOMÉ AND PRÍNCIPE

OFFICIAL NAME: República democrática de São Tomé e Príncipe (Democratic Republic of São Tomé and Príncipe)
AREA: 1,001 sq km
POPULATION: 132,678 (1997 est.)
CAPITAL: São Tomé
LANGUAGE(S): Portuguese

The discovery of oil in São Tomé and Príncipe's waters has provided the nation with a quandary similar to that of a student who's got his first job after university: Do I pay off my debts or blow all the money on clothes and booze?

GABON

OFFICIAL NAME: République Gabonaise (Gabonese Republic)
AREA: 267,667 sq km
POPULATION: 1,308,600 (2002 est.)
CAPITAL: Libreville
LANGUAGE(S): French

When French colonialists Pierre et Jacques arrived in Gabon, they were mighty thirsty and stopped in a café for a drink. "Oh look!" said Pierre, "a little boy will serve us. How cute!"

"He's not a little boy, he's a pygmy," replied Jacques.

"Bonjour, garçon!" said Pierre, ignoring Jacques. "Jacques et moi would like un little glass of wine, s'il vous plaît. Now run along and get your papa, we need to talk to a grown-up."

The pygmy fellow looked at Jacques, who held up his hands and mouthed, "He's an idiot."

Not finding any "grown-ups," Pierre decided to take control of things and erected a French flag and added Gabon to the other bits of French Equatorial Africa (Chad, Central African Republic, and Congo), before challenging some locals to a game of basketball.

CONGO

OFFICIAL NAME: République du Congo (Republic of the Congo)
AREA: 342,000 sq km
POPULATION: 3,396,540 (2005 est.)
CAPITAL: Brazzaville
LANGUAGE(S): French

DR CONGO

OFFICIAL NAME: République Democratique du Congo (Democratic Republic of the Congo)
AREA: 2,344,858 sq km
POPULATION: 42,150,000 (1998 est.)
CAPITAL: Kinshasa
LANGUAGE(S): French, English

The Republic of Congo is more commonly called Congo, or sometimes Congo-Brazzaville. When the French were flouncing around, smoking Gitanes, and cheating on their wives, it was called Middle Congo.

The Democratic Republic of Congo is also known as DR Congo, DRC, Congo (just to confuse people), and Congo-Kinshasa. It used to be called Zaire. Before that it was called Belgian Congo. And before *that* it was Congo Free State.

Now Congo and DR Congo are locked like fighting stags in a one-upmanship contest. Congo is soon expected to become the Really Democratic Republic of Congo. DR Congo's comeback is subject to some discussion within the country, but the leading candidate is said to be the Really, Really, Really Democratic Republic of the Best and Most Loveliest Country Containing the Word Congo.

This week's border sign.

 ANGOLA

OFFICIAL NAME: República de Angola (Republic of Angola)
AREA: 1,246,700 sq km
POPULATION: 11,521,000 (2004 est.)
CAPITAL: Luanda
LANGUAGE(S): Portuguese

Angola's recent history is dominated by a twenty-seven-year civil war. After a coup d'état in Portugal saw the fascists overthrown, the new military government gave Angola its independence in 1975. A coalition of three groups then formed a government that lasted for about twenty minutes, after which all hell broke loose. Cuba, backed by the Soviet Union, helped out one side; the U.S. and South Africa helped out the other. Lots of bullets and half a million dead people later, the civil war came to an end. It's a good job it ended when it did since the western media was dedicating way too much time to the civil war of an African nation that no one knew the location of; and, with the Grammys coming up, people really did want to spend some time pondering what sort of dress Alicia Keys might wear.

East Africa

 ERITREA

OFFICIAL NAME: State of Eritrea
AREA: 121,100 sq km
POPULATION: 3,917,500 (2002 est.)
CAPITAL: Asmara
LANGUAGE(S): Tigrinya, Arabic, English

Oooh, they like a good war to liven things up here. After Italy was defeated in World War II, this former Italian colony was handed over like an orphan to Ethiopia to look after. Cue thirty years of fighting for independence. You'd think that'd be enough for most people, but nope: A few years later they had a barney with Yemen over some little islands in the Red Sea, and another one with Ethiopia over where exactly in the sand the border between the countries should be. Sadly, it goes without saying really that all this has been going on while the citizens of Eritrea are going hungry.

 ETHIOPIA

OFFICIAL NAME: Federal Democratic Republic of Ethiopia
AREA: 1,127,127 sq km
POPULATION: 63,490,000 (2000 est.)
CAPITAL: Addis Ababa
LANGUAGE(S): Amharic

"It's 12 noon in London, 7 a.m. in Philadelphia, and around the world it's time for Live Aid." Meanwhile, somewhere in northern Ethiopia, another big concert was taking place called Death Aid. The country's leading vultures had all gathered to squawk their latest hits in aid of keeping Ethiopia's famine going. A kettle of some five hundred vultures were circling overhead, rocking out, and hoping for more ineptitude from western governments.

The crowd begins to arrive for Ethiopia's biggest ever vulture concert.

 DJIBOUTI

OFFICIAL NAME: Jumhuriyah Jibuti/République de Djibouti (Republic of Djibouti)
AREA: 23,200 sq km
POPULATION: 466,900 (2004 est.)
CAPITAL: Djibouti
LANGUAGE(S): Arabic, English

Adam Ant's mum was Paul McCartney's cleaner. That's got nothing to do with Djibouti,[21] but it's pretty interesting nonetheless.

SOMALIA

OFFICIAL NAME: Soomaaliya (Somalia)
AREA: 637,000 sq km
POPULATION: 8,228,000 (2005 est.)
CAPITAL: Mogadishu
LANGUAGE(S): Somali, Arabic

At the time of writing, and since 1991, Somalia has had no government, just a bunch of warlords in various bits of the country. Lots of secession-type behaviour is going on with several bits wanting independence. All in all, the area's beginning to be less a nation and more like a Horn of Africa–shaped bit of toffee smashed with a toffee hammer. The presence of al-Qaeda training bases, I'm guessing, is making things a bit sticky, too. Very nice flag, though.

SOMALILAND

OFFICIAL NAME: Jamhuriyatha Soomaaliland (Republic of Somaliland)
AREA: 137,600 sq km
POPULATION: 3,500,000 (2005 est.)
CAPITAL: Hargeisa
LANGUAGE(S): Somali, English, Arabic

A giant superstore selling all the Somalia gifts and souvenirs you could possibly want.

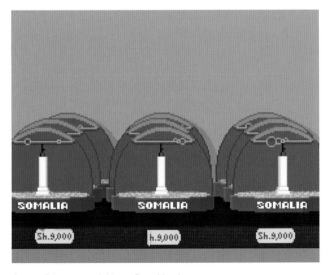

Some of the tat available at Somaliland.

KENYA

OFFICIAL NAME: Jamhuri ya Kenya/Republic of Kenya
AREA: 582,646 sq km
POPULATION: 28,686,607 (1999 census)
CAPITAL: Nairobi
LANGUAGE(S): Swahili, English

Kenya is pretty good. It's got loads of good runners and is a popular location for tourists wishing to go on safari. Indeed, visitors to the Serengeti National Park can see many, many, many lions, snakes, ants, and ostriches. It's like a big zoo without the ice cream.

Fossils have been found of really old people here, too. These date from about two and a half million years ago. One of the skeleton-y fossils was found still grasping a jar of Nescafé, which was still usable and only a couple of days past its "use by" date. On tasting, it was found that antique Nescafé tastes exactly as it does now: like watered-down, burnt dirt.

UGANDA

OFFICIAL NAME: Republic of Uganda
AREA: 241,038 sq km
POPULATION: 24,748,977 (2002 census)
CAPITAL: Kampala
LANGUAGE(S): English, Swahili

Uganda is home to the Grey Crowned Crane. It's even on Uganda's flag. These birds are brilliant. Bored of just being grey and dull, they evolved a shock of gold Don King–style hair, and a red thingy on their necks that they can inflate to make a honking noise. When they want to impress a lady, they do some crazy-legs dancing. It's like Studio 54 all over again. Except in the African savannahs. And without the cocaine.

 RWANDA

OFFICIAL NAME: Repubulika y'u Rwanda/République Rwandaise/
Republic of Rwanda
AREA: 26,338 sq km
POPULATION: 8,128,553 (2002 census)
CAPITAL: Kigali
LANGUAGE(S): Rwanda, French, English

The Rwandan genocide of 1994 was a bad thing. Armed thugs trained by the mainly Hutu government were used to try and stop an invasion by some Tutsis based in Uganda.

The militia groups managed to kill over eight hundred thousand Tutsis and moderate Hutus in just over three months. That's about eight thousand *a day*! The UN sent in a few troops to try and calm things down, and when those troops realised that things were very much going tits up, they phoned the UN to ask for more money and troops. But, sadly, several UN ambassadors were at lunch and were loath to stop scoffing the grilled poodle hearts. When they did get back to the office, they just looked at each other and went, "R*where?*"

These days, though, Rwanda is getting back on its feet. Hutus and Tutsis seem to quite like each other again. It's nice to have a happy ending.

 BURUNDI

OFFICIAL NAME: Republika y'u Burundi/République du Burundi
(Republic of Burundi)
AREA: 27,816 sq km
POPULATION: 6,490,518 (1999 est.)
CAPITAL: Bujumbura
LANGUAGE(S): Rundi, French

Burundi is unique in the world, since it looks like four different animal heads when viewed at different angles: a giraffe, a fish, a pig, and a platypus.

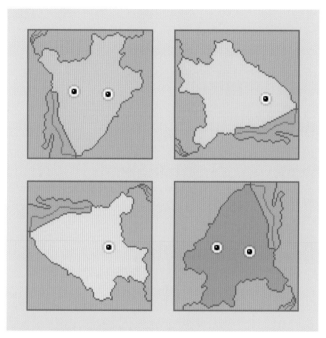

Look! A giraffe, a fish, a pig, and a platypus.

TANZANIA

OFFICIAL NAME: Jamhuri ya Muungano wa Tanzania/United Republic of Tanzania
AREA: 942,799 sq km
POPULATION: 34,569,232 (2002 census)
CAPITAL: Dar es Salaam (acting)
LANGUAGE(S): Swahili, English

The Germans didn't have too many African colonies, but Tanzania was the one closest to their hearts since it was the party colony. It's where they all liked to dance in the pre-*Love Parade* era. And it's how the country's name came about, *tanz* being German for dance.[22]

Freddie Mercury rockin' out in front of Mount Kilimanjaro.

MALAWI

OFFICIAL NAME: Republic of Malawi
AREA: 118,484 sq km
POPULATION: 11,937,934 (2004 est.)
CAPITAL: Lilongwe
LANGUAGE(S): English, Chichewa

Lying in the Great Rift Valley, about a fifth of Malawi is taken up by Lake Malawi. The rest of Malawi is nothing more than the roof of the world's largest Playboy Mansion-esque grotto for Malawi's rich and famous.

MOZAMBIQUE

OFFICIAL NAME: República de Moçambique (Republic of Mozambique)
AREA: 812,379 sq km
POPULATION: 18,082,523 (2002 est.)
CAPITAL: Maputo
LANGUAGE(S): Portuguese

Mozambique has an AK-47 on its flag. And a book. I'm guessing it's not a Beatrix Potter.

ZAMBIA

OFFICIAL NAME: Republic of Zambia
AREA: 752,612 sq km
POPULATION: 9,885,591 (2000 census)
CAPITAL: Lusaka
LANGUAGE(S): English

ZIMBABWE

OFFICIAL NAME: Republic of Zimbabwe
AREA: 390,757 sq km
POPULATION: 11,634,663 (2002 census)
CAPITAL: Harare
LANGUAGE(S): English

Zambia[23] and Zimbabwe[24] used to be called Rhodesia. Before Rhodesia it was called That Chunk of Land with Lots of Bloody Gold Underneath It-ia.[25]

After a while, Rhodesia was split into two bits, Northern Rhodesia and Southern Rhodesia, which, after independence, became Zambia and Zimbabwe. A little bit of rivalry was going on, I think, to see which country could think of a name that'd be last alphabetically.

Southern Africa

 NAMIBIA

OFFICIAL NAME: Republic of Namibia
AREA: 825,118 sq km
POPULATION: 1,826,854 (2001 census)
CAPITAL: Windhoek
LANGUAGE(S): English

This chunk of Africa was colonised by Germany. They'd already grabbed a bit of coastline, then had a chat with some Brits who, fat from gorging on too many gazelle steaks, burped and agreed to give Germany some land, including the Caprivi Strip, the crazy-shaped bit that pokes out east to the Zambezi River. World Wars I and II came along and South Africa and the proto-UN chaps, the League of Nations, took over. Full independence came in 1990 and now the Caprivi Strip is used for drag racing.

 BOTSWANA

OFFICIAL NAME: Republic of Botswana
AREA: 582,356 sq km
POPULATION: 1,680,863 (2001 census)
CAPITAL: Gaborone
LANGUAGE(S): English, Tswana

About 70 percent of Botswana is covered by the Kalahari Desert, which derives its name from the Tswana word *Kgalagadi* meaning "Fuck the Pepsi Challenge, any cola will do."

 SOUTH AFRICA

OFFICIAL NAME: Republic of South Africa
AREA: 1,219,090 sq km
POPULATION: 46,888,200 (2005 est.)
CAPITAL: Pretoria (executive), Bloemfontein (judicial), Cape Town (legislative)
LANGUAGE(S): Afrikaans, English, Ndebele, Pedi, Sotho, Swazi, Tsonga, Tswana, Venda, Xhosa, Zulu

Margaret Thatcher, the former British prime minister, once said that anyone who thought the African National Congress would ever form a government in South Africa was "living in cloud cuckoo land." They did just that in 1993, proving the witch wrong.

Apartheid came into being in 1948 and was a slightly more formal system of segregation than the one inherited from the British colonial days. Like any self-respecting bunch of racist wankers, the newly elected National Party thought it was right to make sure that the dainty white folks never had to come into too much contact with those rough, dirty, dark-skinned folks. So while the whites were gambling, watching topless lasses dancing, and bopping away at Elton John and Queen concerts at Sun City, the blacks were getting the shit kicked out of them by the police.

Resistance by groups like the ANC and Pan Africanist Congress grew, leading to clashes and more oppression from the state. ANC leader Nelson Mandela was charged with treason and chucked in prison; South African Students' Organisation leader Steve Biko was beaten into a coma and left untreated for three days until he died. Slowly but surely, the rest of the world began to condemn the apartheid regime. Economic, cultural, and sporting sanctions were put in place. This didn't seem to bother then-president P. W. Botha. It was only when he had a stroke (I forgot to send a Get-Well-Soon card, I must admit) and F. W. de Klerk took over in 1989 that the thuggery showed real signs of stopping. Within a year, the bans on resistance groups were lifted and, after twenty-seven years inside, Nelson Mandela was released from prison.

So, a dark chapter in human history was over. Nelson Mandela was free, and the world loved him. Sadly, though, his audition to replace the late Freddie Mercury as Queen's vocalist was unsuccessful, and his attempt to become the sixth Spice Girl was a non-starter from the get-go.

Nelson Mandela, Formula One driver Jody Scheckter, golfer Gary Player, Archbishop Desmond Tutu, Thabo Mbeki, and Zulu king Goodwill Zwelethini kaBhekuzulu.

 LESOTHO

OFFICIAL NAME: Muso oa Lesotho/Kingdom of Lesotho
AREA: 30,355 sq km
POPULATION: 2,157,580 (2001 census)
CAPITAL: Maseru
LANGUAGE(S): Sotho, English

Lesotho is landlocked and entirely surrounded by South Africa. It's also pretty high up; most of the country is over 1,800 metres above sea level.

The government of Lesotho is currently planning to build a hundred-mile-long cantilevered water slide that will stretch all the way to the Indian Ocean so that the Basotho don't have to take their passports with them when they fancy a paddle. Exactly how they'll get back to Lesotho without setting foot on South African soil is the main reason why the water slide hasn't been built. That and the more pressing problem of having one of the world's highest rates of HIV/AIDS infection, the prevalence rate of which is estimated to be a damned scary 29 percent.

 SWAZILAND

OFFICIAL NAME: Umbuso weSwatini/Kingdom of Swaziland
AREA: 17,364 sq km
POPULATION: 980,722 (1997 census)
CAPITAL: Mbabane (judicial), Lozitha and Ludzidzini (royal), Lobamba (legislative)
LANGUAGE(S): Swati, English

After gaining independence from Britain in 1968, Swaziland still liked the idea of having a monarchy, so a chap called Sobhuza II took the reins. He had 70 wives and 210 children. Seventy wives. Two hundred and ten children. That's a lot of clowns, a lot of cake, and God knows how many servants blowing up balloons.

When Sobhuza died, his second son, Makhosetive, became King Mswati III at the age of eighteen. Mswati is quite a fellow; he's got loads of palaces and more cars than a BMW factory, spent 25 percent of the nation's annual budget on a private jet, and banned sex for the under eighteens—until, that is, he fancied climbing on

a seventeen-year-old lass, then he changed his mind. I wonder if he realises that he presides over a population with 30 percent unemployment, 39 percent HIV/AIDS infection rate, and a life expectancy of just over 32½ years?

Hugh Hefner feels slightly second rate when he thinks about King Mswati.

REYKJAVIK

ICELAND

Norwegian
Sea

FAROE ISLANDS

NORWAY

SWEDEN

Gulf of Bothnia

FINLAND

HELSINK

BERGEN

OSLO

STOCKHOLM

GOTHENBURK

ESTON
II

RIGA

LATVIA

DENMARK

MALMÖ

COPENHAGEN

Baltic
Sea

KALININGRAD

LITHUANIA

North
Sea

ISLE OF
MAN

IRELAND

DUBLIN

Glasgow
Edinburgh
Belfast

U.K.

Liverpool

Lincoln

My hometown

London

Brighton

NETHERLANDS

AMSTERDAM

HAMBURG

BERLIN

GERMANY

KRAFTWERK

GDANSK

POLAND

Pope JP II

WARSAW

CHANNEL
ISLANDS

BELGIUM

BRUSSELS

English Channel

LUXEMBOURG
LIECHTENSTEIN

PARIS

PRAGUE

Rochelle

Rochelle

CZECH
REPUBLIC

KRAKÓW

Bay of
Biscay

FRANCE

Bonjour

Strasbourg

MUNICH

VIENNA

SLOVAKIA

BRATISLAVA

AUSTRIA

BUDAPEST

HUNGARY

ROMAN

Port.

Bilbao

Bordeaux

Pyrenees

ANDORRA

Toulouse

Zürich
BERN
SWITZ.

Geneva

Lyon

TURIN

MILAN

VENICE

SLOVENIA

ZAGREB

VOJVADINA

BUC

PORTUGAL

LISBON

MADRID

SPAIN

Barcelona

Valencia

Seville

Marseille

GENOA

MONACO

Corsica

PISA

SAN
MARINO

VATICAN CITY

ROME

CROATIA

Adriatic Sea

BOS. &
HERZ.

SARAJEVO

MONTE-
NEGRO

BELGRADE

SERBIA

KOSOVO

TIRANA

ALBANIA

SKOPJE
MACEDONIA

BULGA

SOFIA

Balearic Islands

ITALY

NAPLES

Sardinia

Tyrrhenian Sea

GIBRALTAR

Mediterranean Sea

GREECE

Sicily

ATHENS

A MAP of EUROPE

MALTA

Ionian Sea

FRSBVRG

RUSSIA

. MOSCOW

THIS IS RUSSIA TOO

• Chernobyl
• KIEV

E

Odessa

Sea of Azov

PRIDNESTROVIE

Black Sea

STILL UKRAINE

GEORGIA

ISTANBUL

TURKEY

SCALE 1: 40
HEADS
0 1 2 3 4
0 1 2
TAILS

ALL THESE ISLANDS ARE GREEK

EUROPE

Europe looks like some sausages next to a good, healthy pile of mashed potatoes and sauerkraut surrounded on three sides by an ocean of gravy. Europe is the best bit of the planet by far. Everything good was found or invented here. All the best pop music is from Europe (well, Britain and Scandanavia, anyway), like Aqua, Roxette, and Runrig. In fact, there's only one known thing that isn't of European origin: limbo dancing (and, really, that's not *that* much fun, is it?).

God is European, too.

English, actually.

Northern Europe

ICELAND

OFFICIAL NAME: Lydhveldidh Ísland (Republic of Iceland)
AREA: 102,928 sq km
POPULATION: 293,577 (2005 est.)
CAPITAL: Reykjavík
LANGUAGE(S): Icelandic

The people of Iceland all live on a mountain. They live right at the top because there's a beautiful view. Every morning, the prime minister of Iceland will walk to a cliff and throw things off the edge to mark the new day. The items thrown can be anything that he finds lying around: car parts, bottles, cutlery. After that morning-throwing ritual is over, Icelanders[26] go to work, make some records, become Miss World (even the men), and then get drunk. It's a good life.

FAROE ISLANDS

OFFICIAL NAME: Føroyar/Færøerne (Faroe Islands)
AREA: 1,399 sq km
POPULATION: 48,228 (2004 census)
CAPITAL: Tórshavn
LANGUAGE(S): Faroese, Danish

Situated halfway between the UK and Iceland in the Atlantic Ocean, the Faroe Islands were uninhabited until around 3,000 BC when a bored Egyptian king decided he fancied a fishing trip and went off on holiday with a bunch of mates. It took them quite a while to get there, mind, what with them walking like Egyptians, but once they did arrive, they set down the sheep they'd brought (so that they could have a few lamb casseroles to break up the inevitable monotony of eating fish all the time), got their rods out, and went cod-crazy. Once they'd had their fill they went home, leaving behind a couple of uneaten sheep and a bit of graffiti scratched into a rock proclaiming that "Pharaoh woz ere."

Fast forward to 800-and-something AD when a bunch of Norwegians sailed to the islands, found the sheep and the graffiti, and came to the fairly reasonable conclusion that sheep could write. The sheep then enjoyed a period of several hundred years of being in charge of their Pharaoh Islands until the Danes came along with their fancy Bibles and big sheep-killing knives and took charge. Today, the Faroe Islands are self-governing; although, should the sheep ever rise up and try to reclaim the islands, the Danish military would lend the Faroese people the big knives.

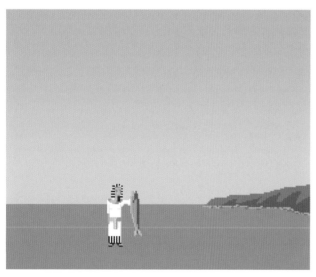

A pharaoh with a massive cod.

DENMARK

OFFICIAL NAME: Kongeriget Danmark (Kingdom of Denmark)
AREA: 43,098 sq km
POPULATION: 5,411,405 (2005 est.)
CAPITAL: Copenhagen
LANGUAGE(S): Danish

There was this Danish prince dude called Hamlet, and he was away at university, sucking on bongs and listening to Bob Marley's *Legend* compilation when someone knocked on his door.

"Dude, your mum's on the phone," said a voice through the aforementioned door.

Answering the phone, the prince found out his dad was dead and fannying around being a ghost, distracting the soldiers from their soldiery work.

Hamlet went home and found his mum had already shacked up with the king's brother who was the new king.

"Mum, what the fuck? Dad's only been dead a couple of days and you're already boning Uncle Claudius?" asked the prince, barely able to look his slut of a mother in the eye.

Anyway, later that night, he's out on the battlements having a sneaky joint when his dad's ghost comes along and tells him that, like *Hart to Hart*, it was murder.

Then the lass he fancies goes insane and tops herself. Then Hamlet goes on holiday, then returns and, for a laugh, digs up the skull of an old court jester and starts talking to it, like a mental person. Then his mum is poisoned, then he does some fencing with another bloke who tells him that indeed, the new king was the bloke who killed his dad. Then he poisons his uncle and finally drinks some poison himself. It was a right old mess.

Horatio, Hamlet's best mate, watches his mate die and mourns his passing by building a Lego statue of Hamlet. After he'd done that, he felt surprisingly well, so he went to the kitchen and made himself a bacon sandwich.

NORWAY

OFFICIAL NAME: Kongeriket Norge (Kingdom of Norway)
AREA: 385,199 sq km
POPULATION: 4,580,181 (2004 est.)
CAPITAL: Oslo
LANGUAGE(S): Norwegian

Prior to the eighth century, the coastline of Norway was fairly smooth-looking. Then came the Vikings. They were a bunch of Norwegians who liked to bomb across the seas in their longships and mix things up a bit. They'd set off, look for some land, then get drunk, fight with the locals, and sleep with their women. When they ran out of booze, they'd go home. By this point, though, their sense of spatial awareness was a bit buggered, and time after time, they'd crash into the coastline. This went on for three hundred years or so, and really messed up the beaches of Norway, cutting them up like the edge of a carpenter's workbench. Today these bits of the coastline are called fjords.

In 1893, Norwegian artist Edvard Munch painted *Skrik (The Scream)*. This made everyone in Norway sad. A nation looked at its fingernails and sniffed back existential tears for ninety-two years until A-ha had a U.S. number one hit with "Take On Me." Then they were happy again.

SWEDEN

OFFICIAL NAME: Konungariket Sverige (Kingdom of Sweden)
AREA: 450,295 sq km
POPULATION: 9,011,392 (2005 est.)
CAPITAL: Stockholm
LANGUAGE(S): Swedish

Sweden has a fascinating history. In the seventeenth century, Sweden had an empire that comprised most of what is now Finland, Estonia, a bit of Norway, and a couple of German beaches, where the Swedes would spend their holidays. It was on one of these holidays that King Karl X Gustav had a little nip of some German beer. He liked it, took some home, and soon every Swede was an alcoholic.

The following two centuries went by in a bit of a blur, until one day a guy called Ingvar decided to make some furniture. Inspired by IKEA, some other blokes decided to form a pop group. And inspired by Abba, a bearded man decided to play some tennis and design underpants. Thus began the Swedish Quiet Renaissance.

While louder countries like the U.S., UK, and Japan bang on about how great their stuff is, Sweden has been quietly taking over the planet with their technically skilled football players and managers, practical and stylish furnishings, melodic pop music, and delicious almondy cakes.

It is estimated that 57 percent of men aged fifteen to forty have had at least one daydream about living with the Cardigans' singer Nina Persson: feeding her strawberries for breakfast while she looks a bit sleepy and is wearing your pyjamas, then taking your springer spaniel for a walk across the fields hand in hand, maybe playing some Jenga on the patio before afternoon tea, reading the great Swedish novels in front of a roaring fire, before retiring to the bedroom to snuggle for a bit.

Some of the great and good (and Roxette) of Sweden: top hit-makers Abba, ace footballer and Calvin Klein model Fredrik Ljungberg, rock group the Hives, football coach Sven-Göran Eriksson, twiddly diddly metal guitarist Yngwie J. Malmsteen, Roxette, and five-time Wimbledon and six-time French Open champion Björn Borg.

ÅLAND

OFFICIAL NAME: Landskapet Åland/Ahvenanmaan Maakunta (Åland Islands)
AREA: 13,517 sq km
POPULATION: 26,711 (2005 est.)
CAPITAL: Mariehamn
LANGUAGE(S): Swedish

Åland consists of a load of islands scattered like confetti between Sweden and Finland at the mouth of the Gulf of Bothnia. It's an autonomous province of Finland but the official language is Swedish.

Creationists, when questioned about Åland's over 6,500 islands, believe that God was distracted by a lass in a bikini He'd just created, and accidentally knocked a load of rocks off the edge of His workbench when He started thinking about creating another lass in a bikini, then creating a video camera and making a film of the girls getting it on with each other. Instead of cleaning the rocks up, He created boats for the postmen to use.

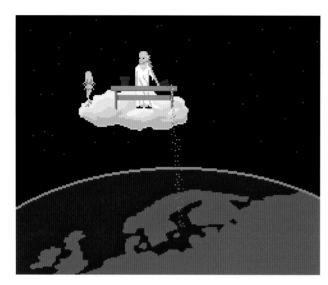

God distracted by a foxy lass.

 FINLAND

OFFICIAL NAME: Suomen Tasavalta/Republiken Finland (Republic of Finland)
AREA: 338,145 sq km
POPULATION: 5,219,732 (2004 est.)
CAPITAL: Helsinki
LANGUAGE(S): none official; national languages are Finnish and Swedish

Finland has 187,888 lakes and is featured in the *Guinness Book of World Records* as the world's largest ice cube tray.

 ESTONIA

OFFICIAL NAME: Eesti Vabariik (Republic of Estonia)
AREA: 43,431 sq km
POPULATION: 1,351,069 (2004 est.)
CAPITAL: Tallinn or Riga or Vilnius
LANGUAGE(S): Estonian

 LATVIA

OFFICIAL NAME: Latvijas Republika (Republic of Latvia)
AREA: 64,589 sq km
POPULATION: 2,345,768 (2002 est.)
CAPITAL: Riga or Tallinn or Vilnius
LANGUAGE(S): Latvian

LITHUANIA

OFFICIAL NAME: Lietuvos Respublika (Republic of Lithuania)
AREA: 65,300 sq km
POPULATION: 3,425,324 (2005 est.)
CAPITAL: Vilnius or Tallinn or Riga
LANGUAGE(S): Lithuanian

To keep the trendy, city-break tourists on their toes, these three nations keep swapping capital cities. Like those blokes who hide a ball under one of three cups, it's up to you to guess exactly where it is you'll be going on your stag weekend.

 UNITED KINGDOM

OFFICIAL NAME: United Kingdom of Great Britain and Northern Ireland
AREA: 242,514 sq km
POPULATION: 58,789,194 (2001 census)
CAPITAL: London
LANGUAGE(S): English, Welsh

The United Kingdom (UK for short) is, of course, the bestest country on the planet. It is home to such greats as "Tiger" Tim Henman, Linda Lusardi, Mark "Rollerball" Rocco, and Ned's Atomic Dustbin. The UK also invented pens, cars, food, outer space, pop music, the Rubik's Cube, and aspirin. Isn't that great? Isn't the UK great?

The UK and its neighbour Ireland share the British Isles, a bunch of islands just off the coast of continental Europe. The UK has four parts to it: England, Wales,

Northern Ireland, and Scotland. The non-English bits all have one thing in common: They hate the English. The only response the English have is getting to the World Cup finals more often.

In the 1960s, the British invaded the United States of America, sending squadrons of clean-cut young men with so-called moptop haircuts over the Atlantic Ocean to re-take the North American country. Although successful for a while, the U.S. regained control of its homeland by deploying the Eagles and the Jackson 5. A sortie by Duran Duran and Culture Club in the mid-eighties was quickly quashed, and the U.S. regained complete power.

The early twenty-first century has seen the UK fearful of terror attacks from an informal armed militia known as Chavs. The Chavs' ultimate political aims are unclear, but intimidation, shoplifting, and alcohol-fuelled teenage pregnancies are common methods of attacking society.

The UK has no mountains and, due to their fatter tongues, its people are unable to correctly pronounce any foreign words that have a diacritical mark.

Some notable Brits include playwright William Shakespeare; war-winner Sir Winston Churchill; Erasure-prototypes Pet Shop Boys; footballer Terry Butcher; oh dear, it's A Flock of Seagulls; horses-and-shagging novelist Jilly Cooper; Scottish singing twins the Proclaimers; Pope-hater Henry VIII; the Welsh Elvis, Shakin' Stevens; and the cast of BBC television comedy show The Office.

ISLE OF MAN

OFFICIAL NAME: Isle of Man/Ellan Vannin
AREA: 572 sq km
POPULATION: 76,538 (2005 est.)
CAPITAL: Douglas
LANGUAGE(S): English, Manx

Built by the Vikings so that they would have somewhere to bomb around on their motorbikes, the Isle of Man is famous for being the birthplace of the Bee Gees. It's also known for its freakish cats.

My sister—a big Bee Gees, freaky cats, and motorbikes fan—lives here, too.

IRELAND

OFFICIAL NAME: Ireland/Éire
AREA: 70,273 sq km
POPULATION: 3,917,203 (2002 census)
CAPITAL: Dublin
LANGUAGE(S): Irish, English

The first time I did karaoke was in Dublin. I was there on some cultural trip with my fellow arty students. I sang "New York, New York" with a girl from my course who, up until that evening, I'd not really liked that much. I thought she was a bit of a snob. But we got on well that night, drank some of that Guinness stuff, and ended up singing. Having slept in the unisex toilets of the hostel, I woke up later that night when some other woman stood over me asking if I was okay. Sadly, rather than replying with courtesy, I told her I could see up her skirt, scrambled to my feet, and went to my room.

A bunch of timid English folk checking out the culture and art scenes of a foreign land.

GUERNSEY

OFFICIAL NAME: Bailiwick of Guernsey/Bailliage de Guernesey
AREA: 78 sq km
POPULATION: 65,228 (2005 est.)
CAPITAL: St. Peter Port
LANGUAGE(S): English, French, Dgèrnésiais

See Jersey (you probably could with some fancy binoculars).

JERSEY

OFFICIAL NAME: Bailiwick of Jersey/Bailliage de Jersey
AREA: 116 sq km
POPULATION: 91,084 (2006 est.)
CAPITAL: Saint Helier
LANGUAGE(S): English, French, Jèrriais

See Guernsey (you probably could with some fancy binoculars, so why not wave at the lass over there with the binoculars? Maybe she's foxy and a good laugh. Maybe her dad is rich. Maybe her mum's good-looking. You really never know with love, do you? It could strike at any moment. But what if neither of you have boats? What if you're too poor to get a ferry? Will your love go unrequited? Look! She's waving back! Better do something about it quick though, sunshine, because look behind you: There's a Frenchman on the coast of Normandy with a massive telescope and he's eyeing her up, too. And he's already got some condoms in his wallet. C'mon lad, get to the chemist and get on that ferry! Run, James, run!).

Western Europe

BELGIUM

OFFICIAL NAME: Koninkrijk België/Royaume de Belgique (Kingdom of Belgium)
AREA: 30,528 sq km
POPULATION: 10,396,421 (2004 est.)
CAPITAL: Brussels
LANGUAGE(S): Dutch, French, German

Once upon a time the Frenchy Walloon and Dutchy Flemish bits of Belgium were at war. The Frenchies built a big wall of balloons to keep the Flems out, but it flew away. The Flems coughed up a river of phlegm to keep the Frenchies out. For ages they were at it hammer and tongs. Then, the Walloons unveiled their new weapon invented by Adolphe Sax, their dastardly inventor. The ranks of the Walloonian armies massed on the border and got out their new-fangled saxophones[27] and began honking. Row upon row of Flemish soldiers keeled over, covering their ears, all shouting "Make it stop!" in Dutch.

Casualties mounted and, fearing sax crimes were happening, the UN sent in a Smurf peacekeeping force who quickly resolved the situation with a lavish banquet of mussels and chips.

LUXEMBOURG

OFFICIAL NAME: Groussherzogtum Lëtzebuerg/Grand-Duché de Luxembourg/Grossherzogtum Luxemburg (Grand Duchy of Luxembourg)
AREA: 2,586 sq km
POPULATION: 439,764 (2001 census)
CAPITAL: Luxembourg
LANGUAGE(S): Luxembourgian, German, French

The fancy-pants Duchy of Luxembourg[28] is one of those tiny nations that somehow manage to still exist in modern Europe, due to EU charters that specify a minimum number of poshos with ostentatious titles before their names. The grand duke of Luxembourg was traditionally the male heir of the previous chap, but in an effort to modernise the process, the heir is now chosen by a phone vote on a *Pop Idol*-style Saturday night television show.

THE NETHERLANDS

OFFICIAL NAME: Koninkrijk der Nederlanden (Kingdom of the Netherlands)
AREA: 41,528 sq km
POPULATION: 16,258,032 (2004 est.)
CAPITAL: Amsterdam
LANGUAGE(S): Dutch

After the Belgian Revolution in the 1830s that led to Belgium becoming an independent state, the Dutch people suddenly noticed that their nation was about half its previous size. Pretty bummed out by this, they sat around wondering what to do. "Hmm, what shall we do?" they all asked. This went on for ages, but a child was born with very nifty fingers in Nijmegen in 1955. He was called Eddie Van Halen. One night, Eddie was sitting in his bedroom noodling away on his guitar—trying out some new tunings and stuff—when he began doing some twiddly diddly finger tapping. What happened next was truly amazing. Similar to the way the universe formed 13.7 billion years ago, the sound coming from Eddie's guitar changed the molecules of air around him, turning them solid. A beautiful mini-sand shower was occurring. After a few minutes, he stood in a small hillock of sand.

"Mum! Mum!" he shouted, in Dutch. His mother was angry at the mess he'd made in his room, but Eddie had an idea. He went and stood by one of the many big low-lying swampy bits of the Netherlands and began playing, slowly filling in the lakes. Four years later, the Netherlands had a ton more land to grow tulips on. Everyone was happy, and Eddie and his brother, Thingy, received a hero's send-off when they got on a boat to go to America to make a band with David Lee Roth.

GERMANY

OFFICIAL NAME: Bundesrepublik Deutschland (Federal Republic of Germany)
AREA: 357,023 sq km
POPULATION: 82,531,671 (2004 est.)
CAPITAL: Berlin
LANGUAGE(S): German

You think of the word *Germany* and certain images pop into your head, no? Good cars, fat blokes in leather trousers, sausages, fat women in leather trousers, Nazis, fat children in leather trousers.... Apparently the Germans are efficient and like things done the right way, too. Their much-loved autobahns are no exception. Even though the roads between all the major cities aren't the same length, the autobahns *are* the same distance, and any excess is simply spiralled underground between the closer cities.

Something that's vaguely interesting about Germany is that there were two ancient tribes that lived there, way back in the olden days, called the Vandals and the Goths. And now if I look of out the window of my office in Berlin, I'm more than likely to see some vandals spraying graffiti on the walls and some Goths mooching around in their huge PVC boots. Brilliant, huh?

Kraftwerk playing an impromptu beach show for some freikörper-kultur *(nudist) people.*

Anyway, German history goes something like this: printing presses; telling the Pope to go shove it; killing a Scottish indie band when they were on tour in Yugoslavia, thus starting a big war; getting an Austrian fella to take over and kill loads of Jews, gypsies, homosexuals, and anyone whose papers aren't in order during an even bigger war; splitting into two bits, one that liked big cars and another that liked big cars but could only buy crappy little cars; reforming again when both bits realised that their love of Depeche Mode was equal; and then they got a lady called Angela to be the boss of the country, and let me tell you, her milkshake certainly brings all the boys to the yard.

 AUSTRIA

OFFICIAL NAME: Republik Österreich (Republic of Austria)
AREA: 83,871 sq km
POPULATION: 8,117,754 (2003 est.)
CAPITAL: Vienna
LANGUAGE(S): German

Austria[29] invented Mozart and fancy prancing horses and is shaped like a chicken drumstick.

 LIECHTENSTEIN

OFFICIAL NAME: Fürstentum Liechtenstein (Principality of Liechtenstein)
AREA: 160 sq km
POPULATION: 34,600 (2005 est.)
CAPITAL: Vaduz
LANGUAGE(S): German

Liechtenstein is a tiny European country squeezed between Switzerland and Austria like a remote control between sofa cushions. Since Hanni Wenzel won two gold medals at the 1980 Winter Olympics, the citizens have done nothing. Absolutely nothing. It can't get any better than this, they all thought, and they decided to hibernate forever. Now the nation is like a volcanic-ash-and-Pink-Floyd-less Pompeii, just with a few Swiss, German, and Austrian commuters making sure the banks stay open.

 SWITZERLAND

OFFICIAL NAME: Confédération Suisse/Schweizerische Eidgenossenschaft/Confederazione Svizzera/Confedaraziun Svizra (Swiss Confederation)
AREA: 41,284 sq km
POPULATION: 7,288,010 (2000 census)
CAPITAL: Bern
LANGUAGE(S): French, German, Italian, Romansh

Switzerland is that most curious of countries: one that doesn't like fighting. While everyone else is out cracking skulls or having their skulls cracked, lil' ol' landlocked Switzerland is having a jolly old time listening to Young Gods albums and watching Roger Federer win every tennis match for the rest of eternity.

Of course, this military neutrality has its downsides. It means I can fall back on lazy stereotypes and clichés without them threatening to beat the crap out of me with their Swiss cheese-eatin', watch-makin', secretive-bankin' fists.

The Swiss people are all orphans. At an early age they are sent to live in the mountains with their grumpy grandfathers and are usually friends with goatherds called Peter. Even goatherds called Peter are friends with *other* goatherds called Peter. All tends to go well, and the Swiss enjoy their childhoods until a bitchy old auntie comes along and takes them to school in Frankfurt. At this point the Swiss often feel a bit sad, and will make friends with cute rich girls in wheelchairs until a doctor comes along, diagnoses that the Swiss are homesick for their beloved mountains, and then they will return home. The cute rich girls in their wheelchairs will visit, though. The goatherds called Peter tend to be envious of the friendships formed with the cute invalid girls and will destroy their wheelchairs by pushing them down the mountains. The Swiss, being nice and fair and not liking violence, will bring together the goatherds called Peter and the cute invalid girls and ask them to be friends. More often than not, they become friends and will spend their afternoons whittling together, making cuckoo clocks, skis, or alpenhorns with their fancy Swiss Army knives.

Some notable Swiss folk: superb tennis player Roger Federer, FIFA top dog Sepp Blatter, artists Alberto Giacometti and H. R. Giger, moustache-y pop duo Yello, footballer Hakan Yakin, and industrial-ish band the Young Gods.

 FRANCE

OFFICIAL NAME: République Française (French Republic)
AREA: 543,965 sq km
POPULATION: 58,518,748 (1999 census)
CAPITAL: Paris
LANGUAGE(S): English

For most of my formative years I had the feeling that I was lucky to be British. "What about those poor suckers who had to grow up being Costa Rican or Portuguese or French," I'd think, "they must be so jealous of us Brits!" This, of course, is completely wrong. But it's a feeling I grew up having inside me. Nobody told me it; it was just there in the air that we Britishers breathed into our lungs. But as I got older, and as I learned more of the sort of knowledge that comes in handy at pub quizzes, I found out that, no! the telephone wasn't a British invention, no! neither was Kellogg's Cornflakes, and no! nor was Scotch tape. But my brain was confused. These things had English-sounding names, therefore they must be English inventions, surely? I understood that spaghetti was from Italy because the word sounded foreign, and I understood that the Chinese food we ate was, er, Chinese because the shop had funny letters on the menu. As this ingrained and internal flag-waving began to fritter away, it became clear that making jokes about the French was a silly thing to do, too. They'd done some brilliant stuff: invented the bikini, Braille, pasteurisation, the hot air balloon, the calculator, and the Eiffel Tower.

But yet, we still take the piss out of the French and make them the butt of plenty of jokes. (See elsewhere in the book for examples. Sorry, France.)

And I wonder: Do the French care? I hope not. I hope they carry on being wonderfully idiosyncratic. I hope they continue going on strike the moment the boss looks at them a bit funny. I hope they continue to protest about any slight on their way of life. I hope they continue to be haughty and stylish. I hope their star football players continue to astound us with crazy head-butts (and I hope their national team continues to be successful, knowing how much it pisses off Jean-Marie Le Pen). I hope the women continue to be beautiful and make me melt when I hear them talking. I hope they keep giving us such talented people as Niki de Saint Phalle, Serge Gainsbourg, Zinedine Zidane, Brigitte Bardot, Jacques Tati, Audrey Tautou,[30] Jean-Luc Godard, Daft Punk, Anaïs Nin, Claude Debussy, Henri Fantin-Latour, Jean-Michel Jarre,[31] Paul Cézanne, Thierry Henry, Maurice Ravel, Juliette Binoche, Paul Gauguin, Philippe Starck, René Descartes, Marcel Duchamp, Eric Cantona,[32] Pierre-Auguste Renoir, Jean-Paul Sartre, and Michel Platini....

Frankly, anyone who can piss off the Republican Party so much that some of them will want to do something as mind-blowingly demented and childish as renaming French fries has gotta be doing something right.

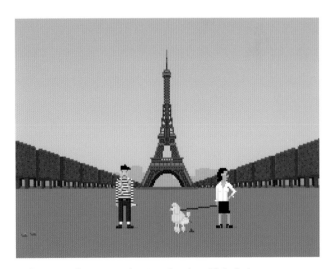

A phenomenally accurate drawing of modern life in Paris.

MONACO

OFFICIAL NAME: Principauté de Monaco (Principality of Monaco)
AREA: 1.95 sq km
POPULATION: 32,020 (2000 census)
CAPITAL: none
LANGUAGE(S): French, Monégasque

Monaco was once part of northern France, quite close to Belgium. In 1962, trying to woo Hollywood actress and future wife Grace Kelly by showing off a bit, Prince Rainer III challenged President Charles de Gaulle to a game of blackjack. The prince won and took his prize: a bit of land on the fancy south coast of France to call his own.

Since then, Monaco has gone from strength to strength, building lots of casinos and exclusive nightclubs and restaurants, and generally becoming a playground for the rich and famous. Not many people live here, though. In fact, the population is about one-third the size of the cathedral city of Lincoln[33] in the United Kingdom. But those who do live here tend to be filthy rich. These folks like nothing more than driving their Formula One racing cars round and round, playing Princess Stéphanie CDs, and shouting, "I don't pay taxes!" at poor people.

The highlight of Monaco's calendar is the Formula One Grand Prix in Monte Carlo. Even when I was racing as Michael Schumacher, I have never won the Monaco Grand Prix on the Nintendo 64 game *F1 World Grand Prix 2*.

Although Monaco is dead small, land reclaimed from the sea has made it a bit bigger. If reclamation continues at the current rate, Monaco will fill the Mediterranean Sea by the year 2417, an estimate that Buck Rogers confirmed from his luxury Monacan villa overlooking Tel Aviv.

The most famous folks in Monaco are the royal lot, the House of Grimaldi. There's current boss Prince Albert II, his late father Prince Rainier III, his late mother Princess Grace, and his sister Princess Stéphanie. Scottish F1 driver David Coulthard lives and owns a hotel there. Both King Farouk I of Egypt and arms-trader Sir Basil Zaharoff lived there for a while, too. Top French footballer Thierry Henry played 118 times for AS Monaco FC, scoring twenty-six goals.

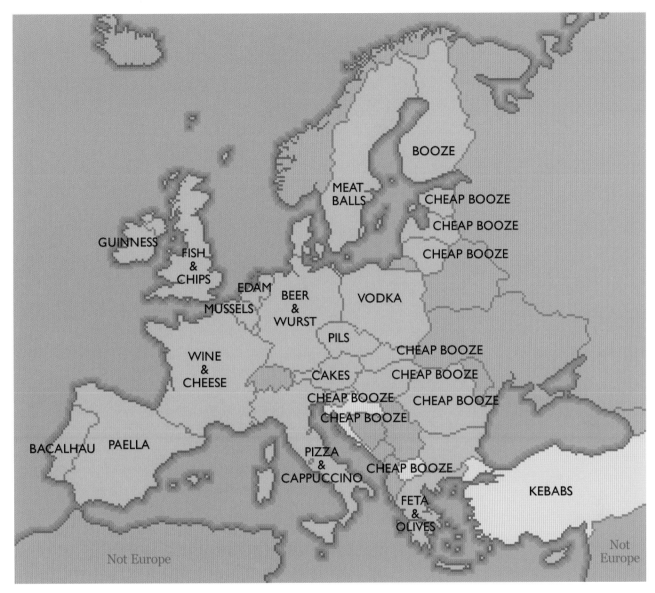

How the fat European parliament dudes see the continent.

The European Union

The European Union is a bunch of countries—in Europe, coincidentally—that all decided they wanted to make a whole heap more paperwork. Bored of only having small forests of trees destroyed for bureaucratic reasons, France, Germany, Britain, and some others got together to have a new government that could invent laws and stuff that would use up more paper. It also means the leaders of these countries can have big old feasts every few months and, wink wink, do some work.

Southern Europe

 PORTUGAL

OFFICIAL NAME: República Portuguesa (Portuguese Republic)
AREA: 92,152 sq km
POPULATION: 10,474,685 (2003 est.)
CAPITAL: Lisbon
LANGUAGE(S): Portuguese, Mirandese

Slotting neatly into the Iberian Peninsula like a laptop's battery pack, Portugal was actually an island until the 1960s, when the new and groovy craze for chewing bubble gum led to an unexpectedly massive amount of rockin' Portuguese youngsters spitting out masticated litter, thus joining friendly lil' Portugal to its big Spanishy neighbour.

 SPAIN

OFFICIAL NAME: Reino de España (Kingdom of Spain)
AREA: 505,988 sq km
POPULATION: 43,197,684 (2004 est.)
CAPITAL: Madrid
LANGUAGE(S): Castilian Spanish, Euskera, Catalan, Galician

I guess it's okay to fancy Penelope Cruz again now that she's not Alien Boy's girlfriend anymore. It's weird how someone's choice of partner can really put you off someone, isn't it? Back in the day, you'd have thought nothing could've dimmed the simmering doe-eyed lusciousness of Katie Holmes. Up pops Top Gun and she's suddenly a bit mumsy and not particularly come-hither-ly. This has got nothing to do with Spain, granted. What do you think this is, anyway, some sort of atlas? You crazy, crazy fool....

 GIBRALTAR

OFFICIAL NAME: Gibraltar
AREA: 6.5 sq km
POPULATION: 27,921 (2005 est.)
CAPITAL: Gibraltar
LANGUAGE(S): English

Gibraltar is a strategically important hunk of rock at the mouth of the Mediterranean Sea, the sovereignty of which is something that is still questioned by Spain. It's currently an overseas territory of the United Kingdom, but Spain wants it back, mainly because they love the monkeys.

 ANDORRA

OFFICIAL NAME: Principat d'Andorra (Principality of Andorra)
AREA: 464 sq km
POPULATION: 72,320 (2003 est.)
CAPITAL: Andorra la Vella
LANGUAGE(S): Catalan

While Spanish and French cartographers were working out the border along the Pyrenees mountain range that runs between their two nations, both made an error in their calculations at around the same point. Looking at the maps, *le cartographe* and *el cartógrafo* wondered what had happened: They'd both missed a bit. Little did they know, that in that "bit" were a bunch of people who were, well, happy about dancing in the fields singing, "La la la, we've got a country! La la la, but we've got no military! La la la, can we borrow yours if we need it, please?"

A Spanish BDSM club for cows.

ITALY

OFFICIAL NAME: Repubblica Italiana (Italian Republic)
AREA: 301,277 sq km
POPULATION: 57,321,070 (2003 est.)
CAPITAL: Rome
LANGUAGE(S): Italian

Italy's flag takes its colours from those traditionally used on pizza boxes and is probably due another prime minister right about............now. And there'll probably be another by the time you get to the end of this book.

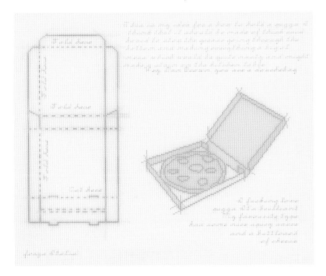

Leonardo da Vinci's design for a pizza delivery box.

SAN MARINO

OFFICIAL NAME: Serenissima Repubblica di San Marino (Most Serene Republic of San Marino)
AREA: 61.2 sq km
POPULATION: 28,753 (2003 est.)
CAPITAL: San Marino
LANGUAGE(S): Italian

Most Serene, eh? A bit up itself that, isn't it?

Surrounded on all sides of its sixty-one square kilometres by Italy, San Marino is one-third of the very exclusive enclave club (Vatican City and Lesotho are the other members). It's also one of the most geek-friendly countries in the world, due to its postage stamps being only valid for use within San Marino and its euro coins being of sweat-inducing interest to collectors.

Here's Tom with the sport: San Marino's national football team was invented to let every other team feel good about themselves for a few hours, what with them never having won a competitive match ever, and the San Marino Grand Prix doesn't actually take place there, it takes place in the Italian town of Imola.

VATICAN CITY

OFFICIAL NAME: Stato della Città del Vaticano/Status Civitatis Vaticanae (State of the Vatican City)
AREA: 0.44 sq km
POPULATION: 783 (2005 est.)
CAPITAL: Vatican City
LANGUAGE(S): Latin, Italian

With an area of less than half a kilometre, Vatican City is the smallest state in the world. Like those men who build elaborate model railways in their garages and wear funny train driver hats, Pope Pius XI did the same in his garden, except he built loads of very fancy full-size buildings (churches and libraries, etc.), and he wore a different kind of funny hat. He built a heliport too, the fancy old rascal.

Below is the current Vatican head of state, Pope Benedict XVI, or "Superbowl" to his friends. Like previous popes, Benny is a Catholic, used to be a goalkeeper, likes to travel, and wishes for world peace. Benedict XVI has also stated in an internal memo that he does not smoke dope, nor does he approve of such things; indeed, he finds the implication of illegal drug use purely based on rhyming words to be "exceedingly childish." He went on to state that he does like soap on a rope, though.

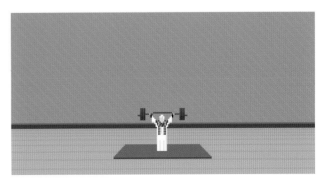

Pope Benedict XVI doing some weight lifting.

MALTA

OFFICIAL NAME: Repubblikka ta' Malta/Republic of Malta
AREA: 315 sq km
POPULATION: 399,867 (2004 est.)
CAPITAL: Valletta
LANGUAGE(S): Maltese, English

The Maltese government was very impressed with Michel Gondry's promotional video for the Chemical Brothers song "Star Guitar,"[34] in which the view from a train window is magically synched-up with the music. So impressed, in fact, that the trains in Malta have been synched up to the song, too. Sadly though, without the aid of fancy CGI stuff, it means that a train journey from Valletta to Birkirkara is a pretty jerky affair.

SLOVENIA

OFFICIAL NAME: Republika Slovenija (Republic of Slovenia)
AREA: 20,273 sq km
POPULATION: 1,964,036 (2002 census)
CAPITAL: Ljubljana
LANGUAGE(S): Slovene

The only artificial lighting allowed by Slovenian law is the sculptures of Dan Flavin.

The streetlights of Slovenia.

CROATIA

OFFICIAL NAME: Republika Hrvatska (Republic of Croatia)
AREA: 56,594 sq km
POPULATION: 4,437,460 (2001 census)
CAPITAL: Zagreb
LANGUAGE(S): Croatian

Croatians are a kind people. Seeing the pain and suffering caused by tropical storms, hurricanes, and typhoons, but also realising that these tropical cyclones were only doing what comes naturally to them, Croatians felt that something had to be done. After a few days of sitting silently in a park, rubbing the bridges of their noses and twiddling with their beard hairs, the town elders of Korenica came up with a plan to give the retired hurricanes a home in a valley in the Dinaric Alps.

Croatia's meteorologists were sent out with a satchel full of books and a packed lunch to find such misunderstood low-pressure villains as Hurricane Mitch, Hurricane Betsy, Hurricane Ivan, and Hurricane Katrina. After months of searching, they found some seventy-five hurricanes hiding in the northern islandy bits of Canada, all looking gloomy and guilty.

"Come with us!" said the Croatian meteorologists. "We know you meant no harm, so we have a home for you!" After a brief confab, the hurricanes agreed to go with the Croatian meteorologists. The flight was a bit tough, mind, what with the hurricanes blowing the sick bags and safety instructions all over the place, but several hours later the hurricanes were safely set free in their new valley home where, to this very day, they blow around free and wild knowing that no one is being harmed. There's a few squirrels that would disagree, but apart from that, everyone's happy.

BOSNIA and HERZEGOVINA

OFFICIAL NAME: Bosna i Hercegovina (Bosnia and Herzegovina)
AREA: 51,209 sq km
POPULATION: 3,789,000 (2002 est.)
CAPITAL: Sarajevo
LANGUAGE(S): Bosnian

Bosnia and Herzegovina only has twenty-three kilometres of coastline, a sneaky little bit that separates the main bit of Croatia from the exclave-y bit where Dubrovnik is. But Bosnia and Herzegovina didn't always have these twenty-three kilometres, oh no. A long time ago (when books were heavy and written by monks, and people played music on flutes and dulcimers) there was a duke called Steve and he was always on the lookout for hot chicks. He had quite a reputation. Tales of his philandering were known as far away as Sherwood Forest. One mild autumn afternoon, he was out riding his horse and singing his favourite song—Foreigner's "I Want to Know What Love Is"—to himself.

Just as he got to the bit where he always forgot the words and started humming, he found himself trying to remember the name of the album that the song appeared on. As any horse rider knows, taking your mind off the road can be dangerous; and so it was that the duke went flying off his horse as he took the corner without due care. He fell down and down through loads of twigs and leaves and came to a stop when he banged his head on a tree trunk by a river.

That was when he saw her, washing her bloomers in the water, a woman of such beauty that it can only be described in the English language thusly: (o)(o)

Steve dusted himself off, lit up a cig, and muttered to himself, "I really *do* want to know what love is...." He went over and introduced himself, but she was all coy and wouldn't tell him her name. No matter how hard he tried, she wouldn't fall for his charms. He tried all his best lines, but she would just chuckle, flutter her eyelashes, and turn away. "What must I do to have your hand, fair maiden?" shouted Steve, as the lady walked over to the tumble dryer. "Two things, duke," whispered the lady.

"First, lend me twenty cents for this dryer. Second, build a seaside resort for me that makes it very inconvenient for most Croatians to get to Dubrovnik."

"It shall be so!" bellowed the duke, fishing around in his trousers for some change. And with that he climbed on his horse and went to his castle to begin planning how he'd complete the fair maiden's second task. He drew a few plans, bribed a few Croats to let him have a bit of beachfront land, then gave his Georgian mate Dave the Builder a call.

Dave was a bit busy, but once Steve offered him a few extra euros, Dave dropped everything and drove over to begin work. Three years later the seaside town was finished. It had a beautiful promenade, two amusement arcades, and a theatre where Boney M were in residence.

Steve rode off into the forest excitedly. Every clippity clop of the horse's hoofs echoed the clippity clop of his heart. When he saw the fair maiden, he dismounted with the agility and artistry of an Olympic gold-medal gymnast. "Come! O maiden, come! I have for you a seaside resort!" he panted. "Come! And we shall be wed!"

"Don't count your chickens, buster," said the maiden, walking towards the duke, swinging her hips foxily.

Once they had arrived at the seaside, Steve turned to the maiden and enquired, "Well? What do you think?"

"Well...it's lovely!" she said. She tried to hug him, but they were still on the horse so it was a bit awkward. "Oh Duke, I think I love you!"

"I love you too, fair maiden," said Steve, hoping that his mates weren't around to hear him being soppy. "Will you be my wife, er, what is your name, anyway?"

"Brenda."

And with that, the sun set on the horizon as they walked hand in hand along the beach.

"*Agent Provocateur*!" shouted the duke at the top of his voice, nearly giving Brenda a heart attack. "Sorry, petal, it's been bugging me for years."

SERBIA

OFFICIAL NAME: Republika Srbija (Republic of Serbia)
AREA: 88,361 sq km
POPULATION: 7,479,437 (2002 census)
CAPITAL: Belgrade
LANGUAGE(S): Serbian

MONTENEGRO

OFFICIAL NAME: Republika Crna Gora (Republic of Montenegro)
AREA: 14,026 sq km
POPULATION: 620,145 (2003 census)
CAPITAL: Podgorica
LANGUAGE(S): Serbian

After the death of President Josip Broz Tito in 1980, tensions in Yugoslavia slowly grew and grew until a full-on war began and pretty quickly got very ugly.

Nowadays, the former Yugoslavia is made up of a bunch of separate republics. Two of those republics united to form Serbia and Montenegro due to their shared love of pop music. Montenegro was named after space-age pop dude Hugo Montenegro, due to the great popularity of his version of Sergio Leone's theme from *The Good, the Bad, and the Ugly*.

The naming of Serbia, though, has a much more interesting story. On the day of the renaming, the whole nation gathered to hear what their country would be called. Behind a curtain, a civil servant with quite a stuffy nose whispered the new name to the president, who went out onto the fancy balcony and pronounced the nation to be called Serbia. The crowd cheered, even though they didn't quite know what it meant. It has since been discovered that the man with the stuffy nose had meant to say "Suburbia," after the 1986 hit by the Pet Shop Boys. Needless to say, he was incredibly embarrassed.

In 2006, music differences lead to Serbia and Montenegro splitting up to pursue solo careers.

VOJVODINA

OFFICIAL NAME: Autonomna Pokrajina Vojvodina/Vajdaság Autonóm Tartomány/Autonómna Pokrajina Vojvodina/Provincia Autonomă Voivodina/ Автономна Покраїна Войводина (Autonomous Province of Vojvodina)
AREA: 21,500 sq km
POPULATION: 2,031,992 (2002 est.)
CAPITAL: Novi Sad
LANGUAGE(S): Serbian, Hungarian, Slovak, Romanian, Croatian, Rusyn

Residents of an autonomous province of Serbia, Vojvainans really can't stand the Pet Shop Boys, preferring heavy metal instead, particularly the early recordings of Canadian thrash metallers Voivod.

KOSOVO

OFFICIAL NAME: Kosovë/Kosovo i Metohija (Kosovo)
AREA: 10,912 sq km
POPULATION: 2,100,000 (2003 est.)
CAPITAL: Priština
LANGUAGE(S): Albanian, Serbian

An autonomous province of Yugoslavia since 1974, Kosovo was stripped of its autonomy when Slobodan Milosevic came to power in 1989. Passive resistence by Kosovo's ethnic Albanians gave way to guerrilla attacks on Serb targets by the Kosovo Liberation Army in the mid-nineties, which brought forth Milosevic's brutal crackdown. Then NATO got involved and started bombing stuff. A bit more ethnic cleansing went on, but eventually Kosovo calmed down. Nowadays, more than half of the people of Kosovo live in poverty, so they couldn't care less about what music the other bits of the Balkans prefer.

ALBANIA

OFFICIAL NAME: Republika e Shqipërisë (Republic of Albania)
AREA: 28,703 sq km
POPULATION: 3,069,275 (2001 census)
CAPITAL: Tirana
LANGUAGE(S): Albanian

Albania has been down to the gym recently. It's grown some big muscles. Glistening, rippling mountains wearing pastel-coloured vests. Albania's aim is to pump up so much that it can form a land bridge over the Strait of Otranto to connect with southern Italy.

MACEDONIA

OFFICIAL NAME: Republika Makedonija/Republika e Maqedonisë
(Republic of Macedonia, or alternatively, The Former Yugoslav
Republic of Macedonia)
AREA: 25,713 sq km
POPULATION: 1,936,877 (1994 census)
CAPITAL: Skopje
LANGUAGE(S): Macedonian, Albanian

Due to the aureogasenithisation of the atmosphere
above the Macedonian territory, the sky looks very much
like a child's drawing, with a big gap between the sky and
the land.

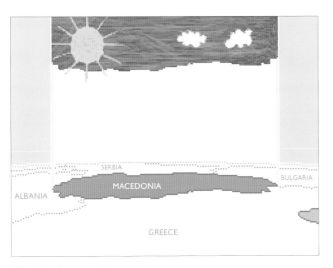

Macedonia's unique sky.

GREECE

OFFICIAL NAME: Ellinikí Dhimokratía (Hellenic Republic)
AREA: 131,957 sq km
POPULATION: 10,964,020 (2001 census)
CAPITAL: Athens
LANGUAGE(S): Greek

Greece is considered the cradle of western civilisation.
It was the birthplace of the beer helmet, 3-D glasses,
white wine spritzers, and that poster of the tennis girl
scratching her bum. Modern thought also has its roots in
Greece; great thinkers like Aristotle, Socrates, and Plato
came up with progressive concepts like democracy, card
tricks, bum sex, and a list of good excuses for when you
really can't be bothered to go to a work colleague's party.
Then the Romans came along with their fancy roads and

buggered things up. Then the Ottomans came along with
their fancy footstools and hung around for a while, until
eventually in 1821, Greeks gained their independence,
and have spent the last couple of centuries trying not to
punch British and American people who snigger when
they see Lesbos on a map.

*Conveniently doing so in a very easy-to-draw meadow in front of the
Acropolis, a happy couple is engaging in some deliciously decadent
Greek sex.*

CYPRUS

OFFICIAL NAME: Kipriakí Dhimokatía/Kıbrıs Cumhuriyeti
(Republic of Cyprus)
AREA: 5,896 sq km
POPULATION: 747,000 (2005 est.)
CAPITAL: Nicosia
LANGUAGE(S): Greek, Turkish

NORTHERN CYPRUS

OFFICIAL NAME: Kuzey Kıbrıs Türk Cumhuriyeti (Turkish
Republic of Northern Cyprus)
AREA: 3,355 sq km
POPULATION: 221,000 (2005 est.)
CAPITAL: Lefkoşia
LANGUAGE(S): Turkish

Cyprus is actually about 50 percent bigger than it looks.
This is all to do with the flag. You see, when the Cypriots
were designing their flag, they fancied having a silhouette

shape of the island in the middle. "All fine and dandy," said Mr. Flag, "I can do that. No bother at all." Anyway, it took him ages to do the olive branches because they were dead fiddly and his arthritis was playing up. The night before the grand unveiling of the flag, Mr. Flag's hands were contorted with pain. He tried his best to cut out a yellow Cyprus-shaped shape; he tried his best to sew it onto the flag, but it just didn't look like Cyprus.

Sad, ashamed, and finding it difficult to change the songs on his iPod, Mr. Flag shuffled along to the town hall to meet the fat dignitaries. "Here," said Mr. Flag, handing over the cloth to a man with a big gold chain around his neck, "I did the very best I could." Mr. Gold Chain attached the flag to the cord and began to hoist it up the flagstaff, smiling for the cameras and trying to break wind silently.

The gathered crowd of Cypriots looked up at their new flag and, as one, gasped at the crappy-shaped Cyprus in the middle. It was a dark day in Cyprus's history. A quick meeting was held in the stationery cupboard of the town hall. It was decided that a new flag should be designed. "But," said one fellow sitting in the corner, smoking a cigar and wearing sunglasses like the sort Elton John wears, "what about these here felt-tip pens?"

He scooted a box of blue felt-tip pens across the floor with his foot. He tried to look cool doing it, but the box was a little heavier than he thought and his chair slid backwards and he bumped his head on the wall.

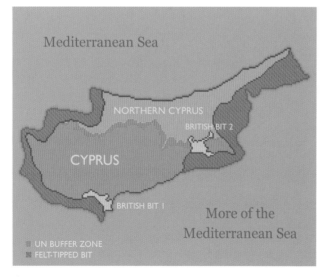

Cyprus: the real shape.

"What an excellent idea!" said Mr. Gold Chain. "Let's get the people to work!" And for the next year, the good people of Cyprus began colouring the fields and beaches of their island blue until they perfectly matched the shape on the flag. Little did they know that not much more than a decade later, Turkey would invade the northern bit of the island and proclaim independence, something that has yet to be recognised by the international community.[34]

 AKROTIRI and DHEKELIA

OFFICIAL NAME: Akrotiri and Dhekelia (Western and Eastern Sovereign Base Areas)
AREA: 256 sq km
POPULATION: 14,000 (2006 est.)
CAPITAL: Episkopi Cantonment
LANGUAGE(S): English

Two military bases that the Brits hung onto after Cyprus gained its independence because it's jolly nice and sunny here.

Eastern Europe

 POLAND

OFFICIAL NAME: Rzeczpospolita Polska (Republic of Poland)
AREA: 312,685 sq km
POPULATION: 38,199,100 (2003 est.)
CAPITAL: Warsaw
LANGUAGE(S): Polish

The German word for bum (the body part, not the homeless person) is *po*. No wonder the Nazis invaded, really, is it? *Poland, mein Führer, ist ein land full with zee homosexuals, doing zee homosexual po lovemaking. Vee must be going into zee Poland deep und hard and giving it a really good seeing to!*

Anyway, Poland has been around for about a thousand years. During that time, it's been reshaped more times than a lump of plasticine in a kindergarten. Then in 1939, the Nazis invented some bullshit reason—almost as ridiculous as my comedy reason above—to invade Poland. A couple of days later, the Soviet Union invaded Poland, too. The Polish government never surrendered, and fought on with the Allies. A shedload of World War II later, six million Poles had been killed.

Then some communism came along; a Polish[36] man became the pope; some shipyard strikes led to an independent trade union and the slow-but-sure erosion of the Communist Party; and in 1989, communism collapsed in Poland, starting a domino effect throughout Eastern Europe.

Some Poles fighting communism at the shipyard.

 CZECH REPUBLIC

OFFICIAL NAME: Ceská Republika (Czech Republic)
AREA: 78,866 sq km
POPULATION: 10,211,455 (2004 est.)
CAPITAL: Prague
LANGUAGE(S): Czech

 SLOVAKIA

OFFICIAL NAME: Slovenská Republika (Slovak Republic)
AREA: 49,035 sq km
POPULATION: 5,379,455 (2001 census)
CAPITAL: Bratislava
LANGUAGE(S): Slovak

Once upon a time these two nations were one communist-ruled nation called Czechoslovakia. In 1989 they had a Velvet Revolution. Seeing the smooth texture of western European fabrics, Goths—and fans of the Cure in general—began peaceful street protests,

demanding black-and-purple velvet cloaks be made available to them so they could dress like proper Goths. The cumulative tear gas–like effect of five hundred thousand people wearing patchouli oil forced the authorities to back down.

Three years later came the Velvet Divorce when the Czech part and the Slovakia part separated over disagreements about the merits of "Friday I'm In Love."

The *O* part of Czechoslovakia seems to have disappeared.

 HUNGARY

OFFICIAL NAME: Magyar Köztársaság (Republic of Hungary)
AREA: 93,030 sq km
POPULATION: 10,117,000 (2004 est.)
CAPITAL: Budapest
LANGUAGE(S): Hungarian

No, I just had breakfast.[37]

 ROMANIA

OFFICIAL NAME: România (Romania)
AREA: 238,391 sq km
POPULATION: 21,680,974 (2002 census)
CAPITAL: Bucharest
LANGUAGE(S): Romanian

Nicolae Ceausescu, the self-proclaimed "Genius of the Carpathians," ruled communist-era Romania with an iron fist for over thirty years. On Sundays, though, he'd use a silver fist. And when alone with his lady wife, he'd use a vibrating rubber fist. And he also had a special fist with bristles for brushing his dog's hair.

Gymnast Nadia Comaneci, football hero Gheorghe Hagi, tennis player Ilie Nastase, bad guy Nicolae Ceausescu, Vlad III the Impaler, and tall basketball player Gheorghe Muresan.

BULGARIA

OFFICIAL NAME: Republika Bŭlgaria (Republic of Bulgaria)
AREA: 111,002 sq km
POPULATION: 7,761,049 (2005 est.)
CAPITAL: Sofia
LANGUAGE(S): Bulgarian

When Bulgarians want to say yes with their heads, they shake them from side to side. When they want to say no, they nod their heads up and down. Is this true? No. I mean yes.

MOLDOVA

OFFICIAL NAME: Republica Moldova (Republic of Moldova)
AREA: 33,843 sq km
POPULATION: 3,999,271 (2004 census)
CAPITAL: Chişinău
LANGUAGE(S): Moldovan (virtually the same as Romanian)

It should have been the best day of her life, but, for Amanda Carrington, her wedding to Prince Michael of Moldovia will be remembered as the day that there were lots of guns going off and people being massacred. Luckily, they were all all right, bar the odd scratch.

PRIDNESTROVIE

OFFICIAL NAME: Pridnestrovskaia Moldavskaia Respublica
AREA: 4,163 sq km
POPULATION: 611,200 (2003 est.)
CAPITAL: Tiraspol
LANGUAGE(S): Moldovan (still virtually the same as Romanian)

Also known as Transnistria, Pridnestrovie is a region of Moldova that declared its independence in 1990, but is as yet an unrecognised state. It's a long, thin, twig-shaped bit of land between the Dniester River and Ukraine. Moldova's a bit miffed at the loss of this heavily industrialized region, feeling like Pridnestrovie's eaten all the pudding before finishing its greens. Crime seems to be a big problem, with plenty of smuggling and corruption going on. If any Pridnestrovian criminals want this entry for their nation improved, I am open to being bribed.

UKRAINE

OFFICIAL NAME: Ukrayina (Ukraine)
AREA: 603,628 sq km
POPULATION: 17,015,251 (2004 est.)
CAPITAL: Kiev
LANGUAGE(S): Ukrainian

Due to its woven willow borders, paper napkin–covered steppes, and its open-topped ceramic town halls filled with butter, Ukraine was once known as the breadbasket of the Soviet Union.

BELARUS

OFFICIAL NAME: Respublika Belarus (Republic of Belarus)
AREA: 207,600 sq km
POPULATION: 9,849,100 (2004 est.)
CAPITAL: Minsk
LANGUAGE(S): Belarusian, Russian

In Belarus a moose called Bruce tried to seduce a goose. Wooing her with tomato juice, chocolate mousse, and his impression of Zeus, Bruce came to deduce that his wooing of the pretty goose was of no use. She was a goose, he was a moose; they could never reproduce. Bruce the moose became a recluse. After years of drug abuse, Bruce was a sorry excuse of a moose. He found a sturdy spruce, knotted a noose, and killed himself.

RUSSIA

OFFICIAL NAME: Rossiyskaya Federatsiya (Russian Federation)
AREA: 17,075,400 sq km
POPULATION: 145,166,761 (2002 census)
CAPITAL: Moscow
LANGUAGE(S): Russian

Russia is the largest country in the world. It shares its border with loads of countries. You might wanna look that up in a real atlas. It's impressive. Something else that's impressive is Russia's history. There were some tsars and stuff, then a revolution, and loads of people falling down some steps. Some bloke came along and had loads of statues made that looked like him, then another bloke came along and was a bastard to everyone, then it got cold and America was bad, then a man with something on his head decided America wasn't

FAT, LAZY,
CAPITALIST
PIGS

COMMIES

Cold War Europe: How they viewed us and how we viewed them.

too bad, then communism came to an end. All of this, though, is nothing compared to the next big impressive Russian thing to come along, something so devastatingly wonderful and artistic that millennia of Russian history pales in insignificance when placed next to it: t.A.T.u.

t.A.T.u is a pop group of two teenage lasses who wore very short skirts and tight shirts and lezzed it up in the rain in one of their videos. One of them is cute and has got dark hair; the other one is not quite as cute, but, y'know, you still feel guilty looking at her jiggling around. They managed to blur the lines between sexy and paedo quite well. They did some songs too, I think. One of them might have been a cover of a Simple Minds song. Lenin would be proud.

Ivan IV Vasilyevich (Ivan the Terrible); big-cocked chap Rasputin; writers Fyodor Dostoevsky and Leo Tolstoy; communist fellows Vladimir Lenin, Joseph Stalin, Mikhail Gorbachev, and Leonid Brezhnev; and pop minxes t.A.T.u.

Eastern Bloc

For a big chunk of the twentieth century, there were a bunch of lands called the Union of Soviet Socialist Republics. It was a union of the Soviet socialist republics, or CCCP for short. They all liked the colour red, vodka, and Lenin. In the other bits of eastern Europe, they also liked red, vodka, and Lenin, so they decided to get together one day in Warsaw and make a pact to be a gang for ever and ever—just like blood brothers—and to never use the letter *K* ever again. This pact also said that "John F. Ennedy is a fucing waner."

A MAP of ASIA

SCALE 1:62

BIG MACS

0 1 2 3 4 5

0   1   2   3   4

WHOPPERS

GEORGIA
→AUTONOMOUS REGIONS:
ABKHAZIA
ADJARA
SOUTH OSSETIA

ARMENIA

AZERBAIJAN
→ AUTONOMOUS REGIONS:
NAKHICHEVAN
NAGORNO-KARABAKH

Kara
Sea

Laptev
Sea

Norilsk

S i b e r i a

R U S S I A

Ural Mountains

Istanbul

Black
Sea

ANKARA

TURKEY

LEBANON
BEIRUT
ISRAEL
JERUSALEM
THE PALESTINIAN BITS
SYRIA
DAMASCUS

JORDAN

•Mosul

Kirkuk

IRAQ
BAGHDAD

Basra

Caspian Sea

•TEHRAN
•Qom

IRAN

Shiraz

KAZAKHSTAN
IF YOU'RE EXPECTING A BORAT JOKE
YOU'RE OUT OF LUCK.

•Omsk   •Tomsk   •Atomsk

•ASTANA

Aral
Sea

UZBEKISTAN
TASHKENT

TURKMENISTAN
•AŞGABAT

•BISHKEK

•Osh

Lake
Balkhash

Lake
Baikal

ULAN BATOR

MONGOLIA

Gobi Desert

KYRGYZSTAN

C H I N A

The Great Wall

←TAJIKISTAN

SAUDI ARABIA

KUWAIT•
BAHRAIN
AR RIYĀD
QATAR

Makkah

Red Sea

Persian Gulf

UAE

Empty Quarter

Gulf of Oman
MUSCAT

OMAN

YEMEN

ADEN

Gulf of Aden

AFGHAN
ISTAN

KABUL

KANDAHAR

•ISLAMABAD

PAKISTAN

Karachi

Arabian
Sea

Mumbai

TIBET

Himalayas

NEPAL
KATHMANDU

Mount Everest

BHUTAN

•THIMPU

NEW DELHI
•

INDIA

Bangalore

Chennai

Kolkata

DHAKA

BANGLADESH

Bay of Bengal

MYANMAR

RANGOON
Yula

LAOS

THAILAND

BANGKOK

PHNOM P

COLOMBO

SRI LANKA

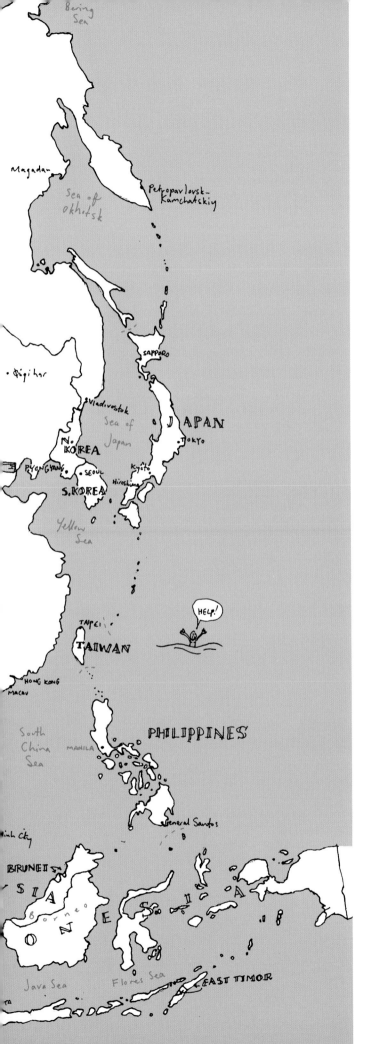

ASIA

Asia is a progressive rock group formed in 1981 by ex-members of the Buggles, King Crimson, Yes, and Emerson Lake and Palmer (the Palmer bit). They are rubbish. But they inspired a continent to form itself out of rocks and stuff. It's really big, too. Bigger than a Big Mac. Most of it is one big chunk, but there's some islandy bits, too. On its western edges it's attached to Europe and Africa, which leads some geography dudes to describe the three continents as one big continent that would rule the seas! Genghis Khan, the Apartheid-era South African police, and Viking warriors taking on all-comers in a no-holds-barred fight to the death! A force to be reckoned with, a force that could crush a grain of salt into a million smaller grains of salt, and then crush each of those grains into another million grains of salt. But for the sake of this atlas, let's look at Asia as a separate continent.

Central Asia

TURKMENISTAN

OFFICIAL NAME: Türkmenistan (Turkmenistan)
AREA: 488,100 sq km
POPULATION: 5,478,900 (2001 est.)
CAPITAL: Ahsgabat
LANGUAGE(S): Turkmen

There's no one more self-righteous than an ex-smoker. Unless, that is, he's also a totalitarian dictator. Sadly for the Turkmen smokers, the late president Saparmurat Niyazov was both of the above. When he quit smoking, everyone else had to quit too. But that's nothing really. He renamed the month of January "Turkmenbashi" (Leader of all Ethnic Turkmen), referring to, of course, himself. He banned ballet and opera, banned men wearing long hair or beards, closed all hospitals outside of the capital city, and replaced the Turkmen word for bread with a word that honours his mother instead. Better not let my mum read this or she'll think I don't love her as much as other boys love their mothers. Since his death, Turkmenistan's nicotine patch and gum industry has nosedived.

One of Saparmurat Niyazov's statues of himself in the ongoing series "Niyazov Salutes Hollywood (In Gold)." Here he's saluting The Karate Kid.

 UZBEKISTAN

OFFICIAL NAME: Ŭzbekiston Respublikasi (Republic of Uzbekistan)
AREA: 447,400 sq km
POPULATION: 26,126,800 (2002 est.)
CAPITAL: Tashkent
LANGUAGE(S): Uzbek

I'm starting to get the feeling that the presence of oil or the fancy materials used to make jewellery goes hand in hand with poverty and human rights abuses.

Uzbekistan has lots of oil and gold, and the UN describes the use of torture as "systematic." Sometimes human beings really do get me down.

 KAZAKHSTAN

OFFICIAL NAME: Qazaqstan Respūblīkasy (Republic of Kazakhstan)
AREA: 2,724,900 sq km
POPULATION: 14,841,900 (2001 est.)
CAPITAL: Astana
LANGUAGE(S): Kazakh

Birthplace of the popular contemporary fruit known as the apple and the bit of the Soviet Union that Sputnik doggy Laika blasted off from, Kazakhstan is best known for introducing the world to the joys of aquatic-themed interior decoration in bathrooms. Stencilled dolphins and fish, shells doubling as soap dishes, and rugs with spurty whales—all Kazakhish stuff.

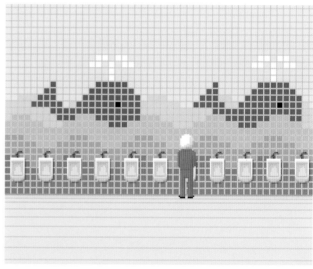

A cosmonaut in the fancy bathroom at the space centre.

 KYRGYZSTAN

OFFICIAL NAME: Kyrgyz Respublikasy/Respublika Kirgizstan (Kyrgyz Republic)
AREA: 199,945 sq km
POPULATION: 4,822,938 (1999 census)
CAPITAL: Bishkek
LANGUAGE(S): Kyrgyz, Russian

Kyrgyzstan is the world's leading exporter of typos.

TAJIKISTAN

OFFICIAL NAME: Jumhurii Tojikistan
AREA: 142,100 sq km
POPULATION: 6,780,400 (2005 est.)
CAPITAL: Dushanbe
LANGUAGE(S): Tajik

About half of the population of Tajikistan is under fourteen years of age. After becoming independent from the Soviet Union, Tajikistan was plunged into civil war. On one side were the grown-ups demanding that chores be done and on the other side were the children fighting for later bedtimes. Eventually in 1997, a UN-brokered peace deal led to slightly later bedtimes, an extra cookie after dinner, and lawns being mowed weekly.

Western Asia

TURKEY

OFFICIAL NAME: Türkiye Cumhuriyeti (Republic of Turkey)
AREA: 783,562 sq km
POPULATION: 71,789,000 (2004 est.)
CAPITAL: Ankara
LANGUAGE(S): Turkish

Turkey is a modern secular republic with its bulk in Asia and a little bit in Europe that was formed in 1923 after the collapse of the Ottoman Empire. Negotiations with the European Union regarding full membership began in 2005 after Turkey promised to supply all EU members of parliament with the tastiest *döner* kebabs, a popular Turkish dish. *Döners* are cloven-hoofed mammals of the *Bovidae* family. They're a bit like goats.

　　Döners are believed to be the only boneless mammal in the world. Its body is solid meat, with all its organs located directly beneath its head. This makes the slaughtering and preparation of the *döner* incredibly easy: Butchers simply skin and trim the beast at the neck and tail, cut off its legs, insert a big metal skewer through the body, and attach it to a rotating spit. They live in the foothills of Mount Ararat and eat only the prettiest

flowers. For many years, the *döner* was thought to be a mythical creature like a unicorn, and the restaurateurs of Ankara and Istanbul created fake *döner* kebabs out of lamb and chicken. But once real *döners* were found...well, you can imagine the tasty feast that was had that night.

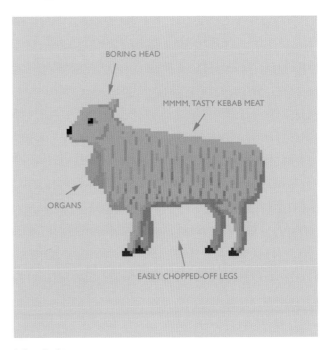

A female döner.

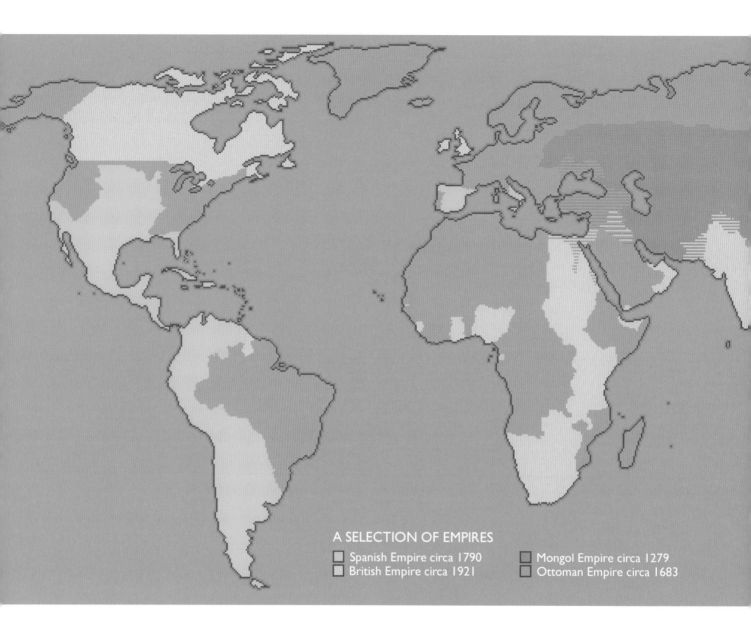

A SELECTION OF EMPIRES
- Spanish Empire circa 1790
- British Empire circa 1921
- Mongol Empire circa 1279
- Ottoman Empire circa 1683

Empires

The Ottoman Empire wasn't the only empire in the world, oh no. There's been plenty of them. An empire is when one country gets a bit greedy and fancies having a bit of something else. Imagine you're at the dinner table, and you decide that the salt and pepper belongs to you. And your mum's dinner, too. And your sister's. You've created a dinner table empire! Then, though, you might try and grab your dad's dinner, but he might give you a clip around the ear, and you might cry. Then your mum and sister will get their dinners back. Empires are something like that, anyway—basically, nicking stuff that doesn't belong to you.

and sucked air through his teeth. A local crone stepped forward and asked if he could knock through a wall to make an open-plan lounge/dining area and put in a patio out the back. Dave sucked though his teeth again, then smiled a charmer's smile, and said, "Well, why don't you go and pop the kettle on, luv, and I'll do you an estimate."

A nice cup of tea and a bit of calculating later, Dave had an answer. "Well, darlin', that wall, see, it's a supporting wall. Can't knock through that, but I could do you a serving hatch, or some nice saloon doors if you'd like. And the patio…well, that's not a problem, sweetheart. All in all, little lady, you're gonna be looking at a five-man, ten-day job, which'll be…oooh, something like 750 yarmaqs, plus materials and VAT. How's that suit you?"

So impressed were the locals with Dave's work that his business went from strength to strength, even though he did have a habit of treading plaster into the carpet on his way to get more cups of tea.

ABKHAZIA

OFFICIAL NAME: Apsny/Apkhazeti/Abhazia (Abkhazia)
AREA: 8,640 sq km
POPULATION: 180,000 (2002 est.)
CAPITAL: Sukhumi
LANGUAGE(S): Abkhaz, Georgian, Russian

Abkhazia is an autonomous republic within Georgia. Having only a thin sliver of coastland, Abkhazians built some sturdy poles (a bit like those that support oil rigs) way out in the Black Sea and more sturdy poles along their borders with Georgia and Russia. Then they attached some canvas to the poles with springs, and now Abkhazians spend their whole lives trampolining. They have the world's only somersaulting army.

GEORGIA

OFFICIAL NAME: Sak'art'velo (Republic of Georgia)
AREA: 70,152 sq km
POPULATION: 4,369,579 (2002 census)
CAPITAL: Tblisi
LANGUAGE(S): Georgian

Georgia was created by a bloke called Dave the Builder. After many invasions over the years by Arabs, Mongols, Persians, and Turks, the country needed a lick of paint. Along comes King David IV in his white carriage (with "I wish my wife was this dirty" written in the dust on the back). He had a look around, took off his crown,

ADJARA

OFFICIAL NAME: Acharis Avtonomiuri Respublika (Autonomous Republic of Adjara)
AREA: 2,900 sq km
POPULATION: 376,016 (2002 census)
CAPITAL: Batumi
LANGUAGE(S): Georgian

Like Abkhazia, Adjara is another autonomous bit within Georgia's borders that has no land, just a big stretched-out sheet of tarpaulin over a rather stinky, stagnant corner of the Black Sea.

Full independence will create a problem, though, as the tent pegs holding the tarp in place are actually on Georgian soil, and, as one Georgian fellow said as he kicked at a peg with his boot, "Oops, they might…just…happen…to…come…loose…."

SOUTH OSSETIA

OFFICIAL NAME: Respublikæ Xussar Iryston/Respublika Yuzhnaya (Republic of South Ossetia)
AREA: 3,900 sq km
POPULATION: 70,000 (2004 est.)
CAPITAL: Tskhinvali
LANGUAGE(S): Ossetian, Russian

Like Abkhazia and Adjara, the self-proclaimed republic of South Ossetia also has a lack of land. This is by choice, though; Ossetians have spent the best part of a thousand years digging away at the many mountains to create a negative version of the mountains just to see what South Ossetia would look like inside out. In 2020, they plan to fill it with jelly and run around on top of it wearing ice skates so the old folks can catch jelly in their mouths like seals in a zoo at feeding time.

ARMENIA

OFFICIAL NAME: Hayastani Hanrapetut'yun (Republic of Armenia)
AREA: 29,743 sq km
POPULATION: 3,212,200 (2004 est.)
CAPITAL: Yerevan
LANGUAGE(S): Armenian

Armenia's national holiday is National Draw-a-Cow Weekend. Citizens and visitors alike follow tradition by gathering in town squares across the land to dance, sing, and draw cows. Each town nominates their best cow-drawing artist to go to Yerevan the next day for the National Best Cow Drawing Final and Parade. The finalists and their own (real) cows form the world's largest human/bovine procession. At sunset, one person is crowned Cow Drawer of the Year, receiving a pair of fluffy cow-shaped slippers, and two pairs of human-shaped slippers for their cow.

AZERBAIJAN

OFFICIAL NAME: Azərbaycan Respublikası (Republic of Azerbaijan)
AREA: 86,600 sq km
POPULATION: 8,075,000 (2000 est.)
CAPITAL: Baku
LANGUAGE(S): Azerbaijani

You may *think* that Azerbaijan exists and you may *think* it's a real country, but no: Azerbaijan only exists because chess grandmaster Garry Kasparov *wants* you to think it exists. His mental powers are so strong he's fooled cartographers, politicians, even satellite photography into believing Azerbaijan is real…

NAGORNO-KARABAKH

OFFICIAL NAME: Nagorno-Karabakh (Nagorno-Karabakh Republic)
AREA: 4,400 sq km
POPULATION: 145,000 (2002 est.)
CAPITAL: Stepanakert
LANGUAGE(S): Armenian

…and just for the hell of it, he toys with us by creating a de facto independent republic inside his imaginary country…

NAKHICHEVAN

OFFICIAL NAME: Naxçıvan Muxtar Respublikası (Nakhichevan Autonomous Republic)
AREA: 86,600 sq km
POPULATION: 363,000 (2000 est.)
CAPITAL: Nakhichevan
LANGUAGE(S): Azerbaijani

…and just in case anyone doubts his powers, he uses mind control to make us believe there's even an autonomous exclave of Azerbaijan.

 SYRIA

OFFICIAL NAME: Al-Jumhūrīyah al-'Arabīyah as-Sūrīyah (Syrian Arabic Republic)
AREA: 185,180 sq km
POPULATION: 17,130,000 (2002 est.)
CAPITAL: Damascus
LANGUAGE(S): Arabic

Syria takes its name—and flag—from a young cartoon fellow called Syri. Much loved by young and old alike, Syri gets into all kinda crazy scrapes. The early, classic black-and-white Syri cartoons were mainly preoccupied with playing tricks on the French: hiding baguettes, putting red pants in the washing machine with their Breton shirts, etc.

In the late sixties, though, Syri's foes stopped being Frenchy and started being Jewishy, and Syri started mucking about with their payos and tzitzit.

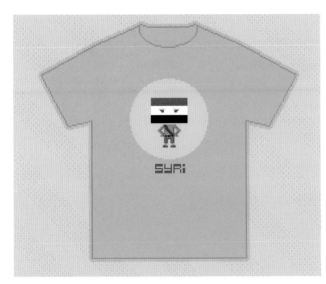

A Syri T-shirt that recently sold on eBay for $459.

 LEBANON

OFFICIAL NAME: Al-Jumhūrīyah al-Lubnānīyah (Lebanese Republic)
AREA: 10,400 sq km
POPULATION: 3,111,828 (1996 est.)
CAPITAL: Beirut
LANGUAGE(S): Arabic

When I was a kid I used to do my homework in the dining room. That was where my dad worked, too. He was an architect and used to do bits and pieces for people on the side from his day job. I'd be doing my physics and he'd be drawing supporting walls. My record player was in the dining room, too, and my dad bought both of the poppy, early-eighties Human League albums, *Dare* and *Hysteria*. We both liked the Human League. The first single off *Hysteria* was called "The Lebanon." I remember being disappointed when I first heard it. After the last few singles they'd released, this one seemed to have way too many guitars on it. And it seemed to be all angry-sounding. At the time, I much preferred the quite flimsy but pretty song "Louise." Of course, listening back to it now, it doesn't sound particularly guitary or angry. But they were good days, me and my dad working away on what we had to do, listening to pop music, blissfully unaware of what was really happening in Lebanon.

 ISRAEL

OFFICIAL NAME: Medinat Yisra'el/ Isrā'īl (State of Israel)
AREA: 21,671 sq km
POPULATION: 6,621,600 (2005 est.)
CAPITAL: Jerusalem (not internationally recognised as the capital)
LANGUAGE(S): Hebrew, Arabic

 OCCUPIED PALESTINIAN TERRITORY

OFFICIAL NAME: The Loving Spoonful
AREA: 6220 sq km (West Bank 5860 sq km; Gaza Strip 360 sq km)
POPULATION: 3,889,249 (West Bank 2,460,492 [2004 est.]; Gaza Strip 1,428,757 [2006 est.])
CAPITAL: none
LANGUAGE(S): Arabic, Hebrew

Oh, for fuck's sake, will you lot just sort it out? You really would think that if God made a city like Jerusalem so important to three religions, He's trying to tell you something. Maybe something like, "Here's some people I'd like you to meet. They like Me, too. Why not have a nice game of football and share some cupcakes?"

Former president of the Palestinian National Authority Yasser Arafat; former Prime Minister of Israel Ariel Sharon; Hamas politician Muhammad Hassan Abu Tir; KISS bass player Gene Simmons; former leader of Hamas Sheikh Ahmed Yassin; former Prime Minister of Israel and one of the founders of the State of Israel Golda Meir; former president of the Palestinian National Authority Mahmoud Abbas; and nuclear weapon "whistle blower" Mordechai Vanunu.

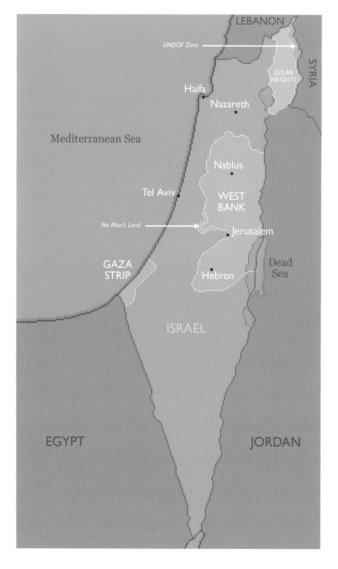

JORDAN

OFFICIAL NAME: Al-Mamlakah al-Urdunnīyah al-Hāshimīyah (Hashemite Kingdom of Jordan)
AREA: 89,342 sq km
POPULATION: 5,100,981 (2004 census)
CAPITAL: Amman
LANGUAGE(S): Arabic

I find it odd how easy it is to *not* associate things which have the same name. For example, I didn't really connect the fact that there are two Apples until the 2003 lawsuit that Apple Corps filed against Apple Computer, even though I've only ever used the latter to do my computing, and some of my favourite records were released by the former. Similarly, until I began writing this book, I'd not thought about a country with a very long history, in one of the most crucial areas of the world, sharing its name with a British glamour model with enormous hooters.

IRAQ

OFFICIAL NAME: Al-Jumhūrīyah al-'Irāqīyah (Republic of Iraq)
AREA: 434,128 sq km
POPULATION: 27,139,585 (2004 est.)
CAPITAL: Baghdad
LANGUAGE(S): Arabic, Kurdish

Must be boom-time in the coffin manufacturing business, huh?

 KUWAIT

OFFICIAL NAME: Dawlat al-Kuwayt (State of Kuwait)
AREA: 17,818 sq km
POPULATION: 2,240,896 (2001 est.)
CAPITAL: Kuwait City
LANGUAGE(S): Arabic

If you squint a bit, Kuwait looks like a side profile of Darth Vader.[38] That must surely be some comfort for Kuwaitis after Saddam did his best to fuck everything up on his way out.

Luke, I am your father, etc.

 SAUDI ARABIA

OFFICIAL NAME: Al-Mamlakah al-'Arabīyah as-Sa'ūdīyah (Kingdom of Saudi Arabia)
AREA: 2,149,690 sq km
POPULATION: 22,673,538 (2004 census)
CAPITAL: Riyadh
LANGUAGE(S): Arabic

What they should do here, right, is buy a load of cement, pump in loads of water, and turn all that desert into a big skate park. It'd be great. They could still make the women skate behind the men, if at all; they could still chop peoples' hands off for, I dunno, cutting in the queue to go on the halfpipe, or, you know, for looking a bit gay. That's what *I'd* do if I was the king. Well, the skate park bit, not the blatant human rights abuses bit.

Sheikhs and their ladies getting rad.

 BAHRAIN

OFFICIAL NAME: Mamlakat al-Baḥrayn (Kingdom of Bahrain)
AREA: 720 sq km
POPULATION: 650,604 (2001 census)
CAPITAL: Manama
LANGUAGE(S): Arabic

There are lots of places that folks think might have been where the Garden of Eden was. Bahrain is one of those places. Luckily for Adam and Eve, God saw fit to build a twenty-five-kilometre bridge to Saudi Arabia allowing their kids to go off and get busy with other people and beget some more kids in other parts of the world; otherwise they'd have been fucked, as Adam had lost the ferry timetable, and no one could be arsed to just sit and wait at the terminal because it smelled of piss.

 QATAR

OFFICIAL NAME: Dawlat Qaṭar (State of Qatar)
AREA: 11,427 sq km
POPULATION: 744,029 (2004 census)
CAPITAL: Doha
LANGUAGE(S): Arabic

The explore-qatar.com Web site states that in Qatar "moments of silence are not considered awkward, rather, a sign of reflection." Most of that silent reflection consists of people thinking, "Really, it's way too fucking hot."

 UNITED ARAB EMIRATES

OFFICIAL NAME: Al-Imarat al-'Arabiyah al-Muttahidah (United Arab Emirates)
AREA: 83,600 sq km
POPULATION: 4,041,000 (2003 est.)
CAPITAL: Abu Dhabi
LANGUAGE(S): Arabic

As the name suggests, this nation is a bunch of Arab emirates that have got together. Seven of them, in fact. One of them is called Dubai. It has some artificial peninsula/islandy things called the Palms, a project designed to get all the tackiest rich people of the world in one place at the same time.

 OMAN

OFFICIAL NAME: Salṭanat 'Umān (Sultanate of Oman)
AREA: 309,500 sq km
POPULATION: 2,340,815 (2003 census)
CAPITAL: Muscat
LANGUAGE(S): Arabic

Arabic hip-hop slang for "oil man."

 YEMEN

OFFICIAL NAME: Al-Jumhūrīyah al-Yamanīyah (Republic of Yemen)
AREA: 555,000 sq km (est.)
POPULATION: 19,721,643 (2004 census)
CAPITAL: Sanaa
LANGUAGE(S): Arabic

When the Oman says, "No, man," the Yemen says, "Yeah, man!"

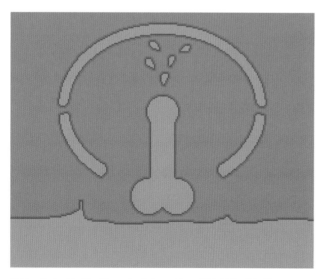

Taking its inspiration from the Palms, this artificial island in Skegness, England, will be completed in 2012.

Southern Asia

 IRAN

OFFICIAL NAME: Jomhūrī-ye Eslāmī-ye Irān (Islamic Republic of Iran)
AREA: 1,629,807 sq km
POPULATION: 67,477,500 (2004 est.)
CAPITAL: Tehran
LANGUAGE(S): Farsi

The 1982 breakthrough hit by A Flock of Seagulls.

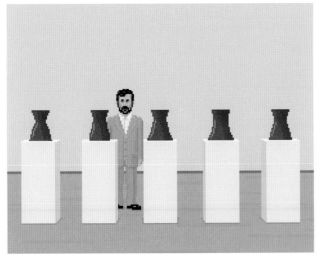

President Ahmadinejad checking out some designs for cooling towers.

 AFGHANISTAN

OFFICIAL NAME: Jomhūrī-ye Eslāmī-ye Afghānestān/Da Afganistan Eslami Jamhuriyat (Islamic Republic of Afghanistan)
AREA: 645,807 sq km
POPULATION: 23,867,000 (2005 est.)
CAPITAL: Kabul
LANGUAGE(S): Dari, Pashto

Afghanistan has had twenty-two flags in the last hundred years. This probably says a lot more about the country than an essay could.

 PAKISTAN

OFFICIAL NAME: Islam-I Jamhuriya-e Pakistan (Islamic Republic of Pakistan)
AREA: 796,096 sq km
POPULATION: 149,030,000 (2003 est.)
CAPITAL: Islamabad
LANGUAGE(S): Urdu

Part of Kashmir currently under Indian control is claimed by Pakistan and, similarly, bits under Pakistani control are claimed by India. Furthermore, there are bits under Chinese control that are claimed by India. None of these nations has claimed the rest of *Physical Graffiti* yet.

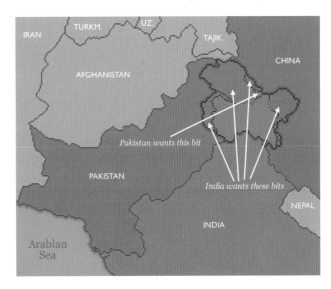

 INDIA

OFFICIAL NAME: Bharat/Republic of India
AREA: 3,166,414 sq km
POPULATION: 1,028,610,328 (2001 census)
CAPITAL: New Delhi
LANGUAGE(S): Hindi, English

India[39] takes its name from a particularly precocious and over-indulged middle-class child who lived in the region during colonial times. British colonialist Peter Anderson and his buxom wife, Emma, would spend many an evening by the Ganges allowing their darling India to run around, poke at people, and ask loudly, "Mummy, why is that lady uglier than you?" Mummy, of course, was not paying attention to India, as she was too busy blocking a very busy pavement with her pram, discussing floristry with another English lady whose equally obnoxious child was called People's Republic of China.

A flurry of prominent Indians: Mohandas Gandhi, India's first prime minister Jawaharlal Nehru, Nehru's daughter and also a prime minister Indira Gandhi, transcendental meditation fella Maharshi Mahesh Yogi, sitar virtuoso Ravi Shankar, Prime Minister Manmohan Singh, tennis player Vijay Amritraj, and cricketer Harbhajan Singh.

 SRI LANKA

OFFICIAL NAME: Sri Lanka Prajatantrika Samajavadi Janarajaya/ Ilangai Jananayaka Socialisa Kudiarasu (Democratic Socialist Republic of Sri Lanka)
AREA: 65,610 sq km
POPULATION: 19,462,000 (2004 est.)
CAPITAL: Colombo
LANGUAGE(S): Sinhala, Tamil

Sri Lanka was originally an island that floated in the clouds. All was wonderful up there for a very long time. People were happy, eating ice cream, playing *Grand Theft Auto* for hours on end, and singing songs of love in the evenings. Then the Europeans came along and saw the shadow that the island was casting on the beaches of southern India and got a bit uppity. The Portuguese and Dutch had a go at pulling the island down but couldn't really sort out the pulley system needed. Then two British fellows named Peter and James came along and watched the Dutch and Portuguese at work.

"Well, well, well," said Peter, wiping his brow and licking his lips at the impending diss he was about to dish out. "What do we have here? Looks like Figo and van Basten think they can pull that there island out of the sky! Oh, you daft Europeans amuse me so!"

James nudged Peter and reminded him that they, too, were Europeans.

"Bother me not, young Jimmy lad, and go and get me a big fucking cannon!" shouted Peter with all the anger of a bull dressed in a tutu against its will.

Thirty minutes later, a rather sweaty James arrived with the required hardware.

"Load that bitch up with a cannonball, then, you lazy tyke!" said Peter, testing James's patience.

Bang! A cannonball went sailing into the sky and landed on top of the island, which rocked a little bit.

Peter instructed James to try again, "This time, though, write WE'VE GOT SOME CAKE FOR YOU on the cannonball."

The deed was done, and Peter and James sat down on the beach and played gin rummy with Figo and van Basten well into the night. When the courageous Brits awoke, they found themselves wallet-less and naked. Figo and van Basten were nowhere to be seen, but the words STUPID ENGLANDERS scratched into the sand could be seen by all and sundry.

This didn't really bother Peter and James too much once they'd noticed that the island was now floating in the ocean and a boat was at the shore waiting to take them there.

When they arrived, they saw a lush kingdom, the kind of place an Englishman dare not even dream of.

As James took some Polaroids, Peter put his arm around the guy waiting to greet them and whispered softly into his ear, "Go and put the kettle on, old fellow, I'm spitting feathers. And give me any back-chat and I'll rip your intestines out with a knitting needle *and* you won't get any cake."

Four hundred and thirty seven billion cups of tea later, the Brits were asked to leave and take the name Ceylon with them. Sri Lanka has been an independent nation ever since.

 NEPAL

OFFICIAL NAME: Nepal Adhirajya (Kingdom of Nepal)
AREA: 147,181 sq km
POPULATION: 23,151,423 (2001 census)
CAPITAL: Kathmandu
LANGUAGE(S): Nepali

Pffff, that sounds like "nipple"! Which is quite apt, really, as the world's perkiest point is on the Himalayan border of Nepal and Tibet. Mount Qomolangma (or Mount

Everest as it's better known) is 8,844 metres high and, were it eligible to play, would probably do very well in the NBA. Legend has it that climbing Mount Qomolangma can make a rich man's penis bigger, too.

BHUTAN

OFFICIAL NAME: Druk-Yul (Kingdom of Bhutan)
AREA: 38,394 sq km
POPULATION: 734,000 (2003 est.)
CAPITAL: Thimphu
LANGUAGE(S): Dzongkha

Bhutan is, and has been for four thousand centuries, ruled by a big dragon. Fiery of breath, scaly of skin, and slightly myopic (he wears contact lenses), the big dragon is called Keith. Whereas once his rule was totalitarian, the 1990s saw a mellowing in Keith's approach to life. He began playing squash, drinking smoothies, and stopped eating red meat. He even bought a Nick Drake CD, which he has publicly stated is "really lovely."

BANGLADESH

OFFICIAL NAME: Gana Prajatantri Bangladesh (People's Republic of Bangladesh)
AREA: 147,570 sq km
POPULATION: 129,247,233 (2001 census)
CAPITAL: Dhaka
LANGUAGE(S): Bengali

This South Asian nation, shaped a bit like a really bad child's drawing of an aeroplane, is one of the world's most densely populated countries. This was a bit of a problem when a couple of European idiots in Range Rovers started bombing around and knocking people over. They got totally mixed up and thought that Bangladesh's capital Dhaka was Dakar in Senegal, home of the Dakar Rally. The tragic thing is they thought they were miles ahead of their competitors.[40]

Eastern Asia

MONGOLIA

OFFICIAL NAME: Mongol Uls (Mongolia)
AREA: 1,564,160 sq km
POPULATION: 2,442,500 (2002 est.)
CAPITAL: Ulaanbaatar
LANGUAGE(S): Khalkha Mongolian

Present-day Mongolia is a landlocked country wedged between Russia and China but, back in the day, it was the centre of a massive empire. Indeed, at its peak, the Mongol Empire stretched all the way from central Europe to the east coast of present-day China, forming the largest contiguous empire ever, ever, ever. That was all the doing of Ghengis Khan who, after getting a baseball bat on a trip to a twentieth-century shopping mall with time travellers Bill S. Preston, Esq., and Ted (Theodore) Logan, began bashing the hell out of people. Bullied as a child with taunts of "Ghengis Khan? Ghengis Khan't more like!" he set about proving his classmates wrong with his trusty Louisville Slugger[41]: first by unifying nomadic tribes to form a Mongol nation, then by expanding that nation every which way but loose. Anyone who stood in his way: Whack! Khan and his men whacked an estimated thirty million people during the time of their empire.

Skipping ahead, and not bothering to explain the disintegration of the empire or anything from the intervening eight hundred years, present-day Mongolians really like the crappy seventies band Smokie.

CHINA

OFFICIAL NAME: Zhōnghuá Rénmín Gònghéguó (People's Republic of China)
AREA: 9,572,900 sq km
POPULATION: 1,262,280,000 (2000 est.)
CAPITAL: Beijing
LANGUAGE(S): Mandarin Chinese

China has a very big wall. China goes doolally when a panda reproduces. China respects and preserves human rights. Two of those statements are true.

TIBET

OFFICIAL NAME: Bod-rang-skyong-ljongs/Xīzàng Zìzhìqū (Tibet Autonomous Region)
AREA: 1,228,400 sq km
POPULATION: 2,740,000 (2004 est.)
CAPITAL: Lhasa
LANGUAGE(S): Tibetan, Chinese

Didn't we sort out all that Free Tibet/Beastie Boys stuff in the mid-nineties? No? Oh, er. Oops, must have got distracted by the whole Blur vs. Oasis[42] thing....

MACAU

OFFICIAL NAME: Aomen Tebie Xingzhengqu/Região Administrativa Especial de Macau (Macau Special Administrative Region)
AREA: 27.5 sq km
POPULATION: 435,235 (2001 census)
CAPITAL: Macau
LANGUAGE(S): Chinese, Portuguese

The unofficial anthem of Macau is "Summer of '69" by Bryan Adams. It can be heard being sung daily by young and old alike atop the steep hills of the city. Although a popular artist in Macau, Adams has angered many residents by refusing to offer more details about his summer of 1969. A letter-writing campaign regarding the topic in 1997 brought only polite rejections from Adams, his fan club, and record label. The main points that the Macanese require answers for are:

- What is the name and location of the five-and-dime store where you bought your first real six-string?

- You played until your fingers bled; did you have to go to the hospital?

- Why did Jimmy quit?

- Did Jody get married in a church? Is he still together with his wife? Is she pretty? Can we see a photo of her, please?

- Do you still believe they were the best days of your life? We only ask because we'd have thought that recording "All for Love" with Rod Stewart and Sting must've been a very good day, too.

HONG KONG

OFFICIAL NAME: Xianggang Tebie Xingzhengqu/Hong Kong Special Administrative Region of the People's Republic of China
AREA: 1,102 sq km
POPULATION: 6,708,389 (2001 census)
CAPITAL: none
LANGUAGE(S): Chinese, English

King Kong's more financially astute brother.

TAIWAN

OFFICIAL NAME: Zhōnghuá Mínguó (Republic of China)
AREA: 36,188 sq km
POPULATION: 22,689,122 (2005 est.)
CAPITAL: Taipei
LANGUAGE(S): Mandarin Chinese

Taiwan (Republic of China) is claimed by China (People's Republic of China). Taiwan views itself as an independent state. Just in case the PRC gets a bit shirty, though, the Taiwanese have built two massive paddles[43] on the sides of the island so they can sail away.

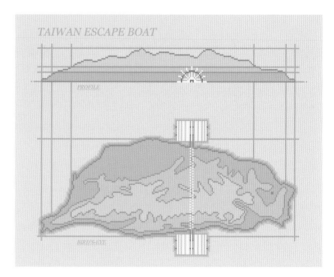

The plans for the escape boat.

NORTH KOREA

OFFICIAL NAME: Chosŏn Minjujuǔi In'mn Konghwaguk
(Democratic People's Republic of Korea)
AREA: 122,762 sq km
POPULATION: 20,522,350 (1993 est.)
CAPITAL: P'yŏngyang
LANGUAGE(S): Korean

SOUTH KOREA

OFFICIAL NAME: Taehan Min'guk (Republic of Korea)
AREA: 99,601 sq km
POPULATION: 46,136,101 (2000 census)
CAPITAL: Seoul
LANGUAGE(S): Korean

The two nations on the Korean peninsula used to be one country. Invaded and occupied by Japan in 1910, Korea was split in half when the Soviet Union and United States defeated Japan at the end of World War II and agreed to each administer their bits of Korea for a while. During that period both the USSR and U.S. eased in governments that were on the same wavelength: a communist government in the north, and an anti-communist government in the south. Both sides thought that they should run the whole of Korea. There was a dramatic clap of thunder, some charts and maps and plans of attack were drawn up, and two million dead people later, a truce kinda left us with virtually the same borders as before the barney started.

Nowadays there's a Demilitarised Zone between the two nations where squirrels can hunt for landmines.

The fortunes of North and South Korea have been *slightly* different since the split in 1948. South Korea is one of those fancy techie nations and has one of the largest economies in the world. North Korea on the other hand has food shortages and its government spends about a quarter of the money it does have on tanks and DVD box sets. While an estimated 150,000 North Koreans are detained in prison camps, an estimated 150,000 South Koreans will be married by Sun Myung Moon.

And while South Korea has hosted the 1988 summer Olympics and cohosted the 2002 World Cup, North Korea has some gymnasts doing a big show now and again. Mainly those gymnastic shows are to celebrate something like North Korean leader Kim Jong-Il's

birthday. He likes a big show. And a drink. He's also building an underground statue of himself out of gold with spectacles made of huge sheets of diamonds and arms held high giving the finger to the rest of the word. Both of those fingers contain nuclear warheads.

Kim Jong-Il's underground gold statue.

JAPAN

OFFICIAL NAME: Nihon (Japan)
AREA: 377,873 sq km
POPULATION: 127,687,000 (2004 est.)
CAPITAL: Tokyo
LANGUAGE(S): Japanese

The name Japan means "cute electronic toy." Japan was created in 660 BC by one of the Sun Goddess's children's children. She said, "Listen here, my boy, go down there to that bit near China and make some big swords and some very neat gardens." Emperor Jimmu, for it was he, replied, "Oh, bloody hell, do I have to? I'm playing *Super Mario 64* and I've nearly beaten Bowser in the Sky!"

The Sun Goddess was adamant, so Jimmu stomped down to earth and chopped up some fish into pretty shapes to stop himself from getting bored. Then he had some fights and invented judo and karate. Then he ate loads of the pretty fish stuff and had a fight with another fat bloke in his underpants and invented sumo.

Fast forward past a load of fighting with China and

Russia, and Imperial Japan was ready to join up with the Nazis and Mussolini's Italy kick-off in World War II, invading and occupying some of the Allies' Asian colonies, then dropping some bombs onto an American naval base. This really ticked off the Americans, who decided to bring things to a stop once and for all by dropping some big, smelly bombs on Hiroshima and Nagasaki, killing 214,000 people. Unsurprisingly, Japan surrendered.

Modern life in Japan is very exciting. Everything is made from computery, electronicy wizardry, even food; the toilets are clever, all the girls are cute, and the men have their penises pixillated at birth just in case they want to be in porn films.

Some Japanese people who failed to get jobs at the Ministry of Cuteness: Cold Boy, Stripey-legged Girl, Jam Sandwich Man, the Honeycomb Brothers, Captain Plump, and One-armed Bunny.

Southeast Asia

MYANMAR

OFFICIAL NAME: Pyidaungzu Myanma Naingngandaw (Union of Myanmar)
AREA: 676,577 sq km
POPULATION: 43,922,000 (1994 est.)
CAPITAL: Yangôn
LANGUAGE(S): Burmese

Myanmar used to be called Burma, and still is by a lot of foreign governments and media organisations. After a long time doing its own thing, Burma became a British colony. After World War II, a fella called Aung San began negotiations for independence. About six months before independence came, Aung San was assassinated by a bunch of his rivals. A couple of military coups later, and the year was 1989. While the rest of the world was shuffling around on the dance floor, grooving away to the Stone Roses, Burma was having an election which gave the party of Aung San's daughter, Aung San Suu Kyi, a comprehensive victory. The outgoing government—the ominously named State Law and Order Restoration Council (SLORC)—decided that they didn't want to be outgoing in the slightest.

So they arrested Aung San Suu Kyi. The rest of the world huffed and puffed and said, "Ooh, that's wrong." The SLORC blew the world a raspberry, changed the name of the country, and has kept Aung San Suu Kyi in prison or under house arrest for virtually the whole time since then. At the time of writing, she's still under house arrest, and I'm still shuffling around in my carpet slippers to the Stone Roses.

THAILAND

OFFICIAL NAME: Muang Thai/Prathet Thai (Kingdom of Thailand)
AREA: 513,120 sq km
POPULATION: 62,799,872 (2002 est.)
CAPITAL: Bangkok
LANGUAGE(S): Thai

Bangkok, or Krung Thep Maha Nakhon Amon Rattanakosin Mahinthara Ayutthaya Mahadilok Phop Noppharat Ratchathani Burirom Udom Ratchaniwet Mahasathan Amon Phiman Awatan Sathit Sakkathattiya

Witsanu Kamprasit to give it its full title, is slowly sinking about five centimetres a year. Civil engineers believe this is due to the unexpected amount of white European travellers traipsing around their city looking for trinkets. This in itself isn't the problem; the problem is the number of these backpackers who have inappropriately thick, manky dreadlocks that create a few extra pounds per square inch of pressure on the city's landscape.

 LAOS

OFFICIAL NAME: Sathalanalat Paxathipatai Paxaxôn Lao (Lao People's Democratic Republic)
AREA: 236,800 sq km
POPULATION: 4,605,300 (1996 est.)
CAPITAL: Vientiane
LANGUAGE(S): Lao

Nestled sweetly between Vietnam and Thailand, Laos has the most elephants in the world. Estimates suggest there are about a million of the buggers roaming around the mountains that make up the majority of Laos.

The French arrived in the nineteenth century and had a jolly old time until 1954 when they ran out of jam and decided to go back home. A long civil war followed when the royalists and communists saw how many jars the French had left behind. Refusing to do anything as menial as cleaning them and taking them to be recycled, the royalists told the communists to get the Fairy Liquid out and stop moaning. The communists, meanwhile, figured they were being oppressed and picked up their weapons instead.

The communists won 3–2 after extra time.

 CAMBODIA

OFFICIAL NAME: Preah Reach Ana Pak Kampuchea (Kingdom of Cambodia)
AREA: 181,035 sq km
POPULATION: 13,542,410 (2004 est.)
CAPITAL: Phnom Penh
LANGUAGE(S): Khmer

For quite a long time Cambodia was at the centre of the Khmer Empire that encompassed parts of modern day Laos, Thailand, and Vietnam. The *les bleus* came along and colonised the whole area in the mid-nineteenth century. Post-colonial Cambodia's headline news was the reign

of the Khmer Rouge. After a civil war in the seventies, the Khmer Rouge leader and the new Prime Minister of Cambodia, Pol Pot, began his campaign of restructuring the country. This meant killing an estimated 1.7 million people: one in four of its citizens. His main targets were monks, cripples, ethnic minorities, intellectuals (especially those educated in the West), and anyone who looked a bit "bookish," leaving Cambodia with a demographic that Fox News can only dream of. Sadly for the human race, Pol Pot escaped punishment, apparently dying of a heart attack in 1998. I hope it fucking hurt, cunt.

 VIETNAM

OFFICIAL NAME: Cong Hoa Xa Hoi Chu Nghia Viet Nam (Socialist Republic of Vietnam)
AREA: 329,241 sq km
POPULATION: 82,069,800 (2004 est.)
CAPITAL: Hanoi
LANGUAGE(S): Vietnamese

Y'know, there really should be some movies about the Vietnam War. Maybe forty fucking thousand of them. All using music by the Doors.[44]

 MALAYSIA

OFFICIAL NAME: Malaysia
AREA: 329,847 sq km
POPULATION: 23,274,690 (2000 census)
CAPITAL: Kuala Lumpur
LANGUAGE(S): Malay

Truly Asia. Not like the other bits of Asia, which are all rubbish.

 BRUNEI

OFFICIAL NAME: Negara Brunei Darussalam (State of Brunei, Abode of Peace)
AREA: 5,765 sq km
POPULATION: 348,800 (2003 est.)
CAPITAL: Bandar Seri Begawan
LANGUAGE(S): Malay

Brunei is a tiny bit of the island of Borneo. It's so tiny that the current sultan makes up for it in two ways: first, by having a massive name, His Majesty Paduka Seri Baginda Sultan Haji Hassanal Bolkiah Mu'izzaddin Waddaulah,

GCB; second, by being really, really rich. He's so rich that he phones up Queen Elizabeth II now and again just to fart into the receiver when she answers. His younger brother Prince Jefri also likes a good bit of puerile humour: He called his fifty-metre-long yacht *Tits*. Yes, *Tits*. *Tits*'s lifeboats are called *Nipple I* and *Nipple II*. I wish I could tell you that this was a joke I made up but it's not.

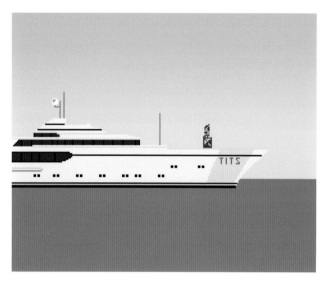

The Sultan of Brunei on his brother's boat.

SINGAPORE

OFFICIAL NAME: Hsin-chia-p'o Kung-ho-kuo/Republik Singapura/ Singapore Kudiyarasu/Republic of Singapore
AREA: 699 sq km
POPULATION: 4,240,300 (2004 est.)
CAPITAL: Singapore
LANGUAGE(S): Chinese, Malay, Tamil, English

Back in time, way before calendars and *Big Brother*, there was a creature called a merlion. The merlion had the head of a lion and the body of a mermaid. It lived in the South China Sea and would come to the shore every night and sing a haunting melody. Locals were hypnotised by the merlion's melody. Others were hypnotised by its beauty. A few were just looking at its boobs.

In times of national crisis, the people of the Singapore islands would gather on the beach and ask the merlion for advice. "Oh great merlion, shall we let the British make us a colony of their empire? Oh great merlion, shall we tell the British that the Japanese are coming to kick their asses? Oh great merlion, shall we adopt the political system of a unicameral parliamentary government?"

The merlion would rear up on its flipper thing and do a big roar for she did not speak English, Chinese, Malay, or Tamil and understood not a jot of what they were saying, and was actually a bit freaked out by all those people staring at her.

The merlion came to be when God and his mates Jimmy and Titch were having a cigarette break, and they decided to play a quick game of Exquisite Corpse. God drew a lion's head (He was pretty good at drawing), Jimmy drew some boobs, and Titch drew a fish tail.

INDONESIA

OFFICIAL NAME: Republik Indonesia (Republic of Indonesia)
AREA: 1,890,754 sq km
POPULATION: 206,264,595 (2000 census)
CAPITAL: Jakarta
LANGUAGE(S): Indonesian

Indonesia has 18,108 islands. Eighteen thousand one hundred and eight! There's Borneo, Timor, and New Guinea, the islands they share with other countries; Krakatoa, the one with the pop star volcano, known locally as Lava Elvis; there's Java, where coffee shops are born, presumably; and Belitung, where they make pepper and jokingly refer to the island as Indo-sneeze-ia. Kakaban, one of the Derawan Islands, has a big lake in the middle called Jellyfish Lake; Simeulue was the island closest to the epicentre of the 2004 Indian Ocean earthquake; and Thousand Islands is a chain of 105 islands that thinks it's better than it is. The island of Flores is where paleoanthropologists found a skeleton of a *Homo floresiensis*, a small olden-days version of a human; Bali you know about; Komodo has the dragons; pfff, what else is there? Oh yes, the Maluku Islands, also know as the Spice Islands: Ginger, Sporty, Scary, Baby, and Posh.

TIMOR-LESTE

OFFICIAL NAME: República Demokrátika Timor Lorosa'e/ República Democrática de Timor-Leste (Democratic Republic of Timor-Leste)
AREA: 14,609 sq km
POPULATION: 1,040,880 (2005 est.)
CAPITAL: Dili
LANGUAGE(S): Tetum, Portuguese

Timor-Leste, often known by its old name East Timor, was a Portuguese colony back in the days when that sort of thing went on. A few rumbles with the Dutch and the Japanese invasion during World War II aside, Portugal held onto Timor until 1975, when it gained independence and became the Democratic Republic of East Timor. For a couple of weeks all was rosy. Then U.S. President Gerald Ford and Secretary of State Henry Kissinger stopped by Indonesia for a little chat with Indonesia's military dictator, General Suharto. No sooner had Ford and Kissinger opened their packets of complimentary peanuts

on Air Force One, than Indonesian forces were rumbling into East Timor, where they stayed for twenty-five years, killing as many as two hundred thousand East Timorese with weapons sold to them by the U.S. and UK.[45]

Anyway, I digress. In 1999, a referendum was planned in East Timor to decide if its citizens wanted to stay part of Indonesia or fly solo. They voted for the latter. Indonesia accepted the result graciously by driving thousands of people from their homes and trashing the joint. Not until Bill Clinton finally told the Indonesian government that he wouldn't sell them any more bullets if they didn't stop behaving like twats did the forces pull out. The UN took on the task of helping the East Timorese form an independent nation, which they finally did in April 2002, becoming the twenty-first century's first new nation.

PHILIPPINES

OFFICIAL NAME: Republika ng Pilipinas/Republic of the Philippines
AREA: 316,294 sq km
POPULATION: 76,498,735 (2000 census)
CAPITAL: Manila
LANGUAGE(S): Filipino, English

The Philippines is the only country in the world where the capital city's buildings are made of beige card stock.

Manila, made of manila folders.

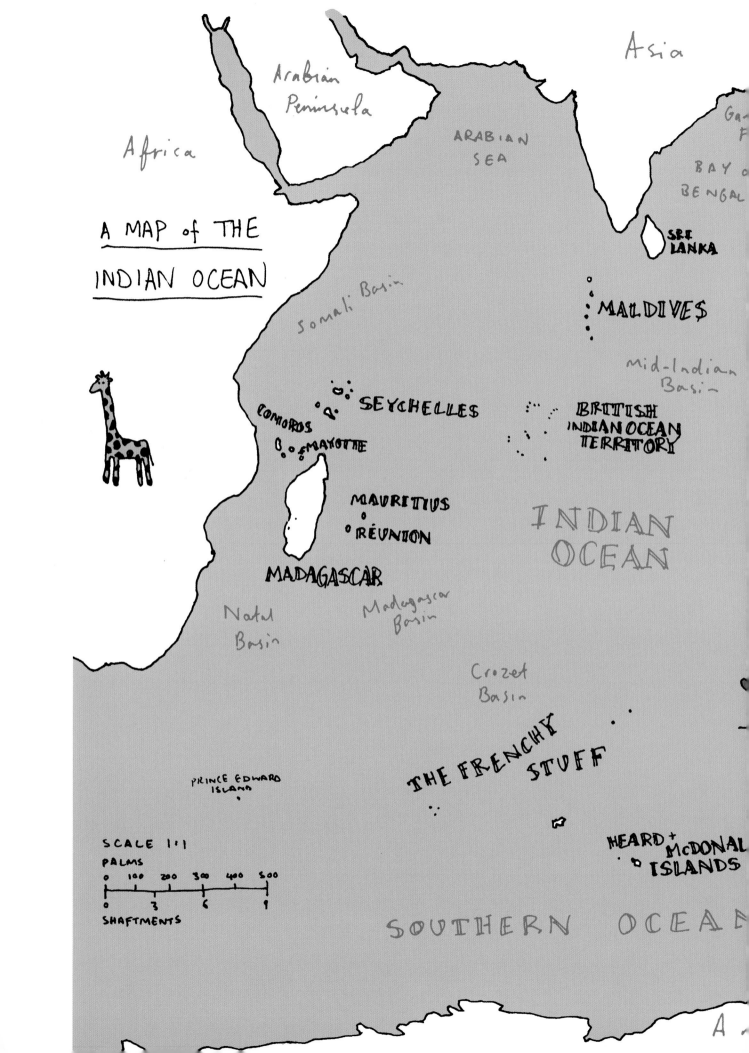

INDIAN OCEAN

Like most oceans, the Indian Ocean is full of water. It goes from the southern tip of Africa to Tasmania and laps against all the coastlines of eastern Africa, southern Asia, and western Australia along the way. Lots of things live in the Indian Ocean. Most of them can be eaten, which is good for nonvegetarians and sushi lovers. Once Europeans had managed to build boats that could sail all the way around the bottom of Africa, it was like permanent rush hour on the Indian Ocean with loads of people going back and forth, collecting souvenirs and tea from the colonies. All the fun stopped, though, in 2004, when a massive earthquake off the coast of Sumatra, Indonesia created a tsunami that really buggered things up all across the ocean and its coastal areas, killing nigh on three hundred thousand people. The earthquake gods obviously didn't realise it was Boxing Day and doing a tsunami would really bum us all out.

 ## SEYCHELLES

OFFICIAL NAME: Repiblik Sesel/Republic of Seychelles/
République des Seychelles
AREA: 455 sq km
POPULATION: 81,200 (2001 est.)
CAPITAL: Victoria
LANGUAGE(S): Seychellois Creole, English, French

Seychelles is the only nation in the world to have a flag designed by an eight-year-old child using some poster paint and a ruler.

 ## COMOROS

OFFICIAL NAME: L'Union des Comores/Udzima wa Komori
(Union of the Comoros)
AREA: 1,862 sq km
POPULATION: 590,200 (2003 census)
CAPITAL: Moroni
LANGUAGE(S): Comorian, Arabic, French

This cluster of islands lying between mainland Africa and Madagascar came about its name in a most peculiar fashion. As a boat full of Frenchmen were bombing around the Indian Ocean colonising whatever was available, two of them were playing Scrabble on the deck. Pierre, the senior of the two, laid down the word "Comores" and began totting up the points in his head. Jacques was not happy. He threw his beret to the ground and said loads of stuff that I can't translate. "Come, come, Jacques," said Pierre playing with his waxy moustache, "for it is the name of those islands yonder!" He dramatically pointed out to sea. Jacques was fuming. He knew that proper nouns weren't allowed, but fearing that further protesting would get him in trouble, he let it go. About twenty minutes later, they landed on the island and Pierre announced, rather sheepishly, to his fellow shipmates, "C'est la Comores!"

MAYOTTE

OFFICIAL NAME: Mayotte
AREA: 374 sq km
POPULATION: 201,234 (2006 est.)
CAPITAL: Mamoudzou
LANGUAGE(S): French

…and when the Comoros decided to cede from its Frenchiness, the people of Mayotte—geographically a part of said islands—turned around and said, "Non! We like being French, because they have the best-looking women and the world's best bicycle race!"

MADAGASCAR

OFFICIAL NAME: Repoblikan'i Madagasikara/République de Madagascar (Republic of Madagascar)
AREA: 587,051 sq km
POPULATION: 15,692,034 (2001 est.)
CAPITAL: Antananarivo
LANGUAGE(S): Malagasy, French

Aaah, it's brilliant. Chris Rock is a donkey, right, and get this, the guy off *Friends* who got to snog Jennifer Aniston is this really sorta hypochondriac giraffe…man, it's dead funny. But enough shitting around: Madagascar is the fourth biggest island in the world (after Great Britain, Spain, and Manhattan), and there's gazillions of animals there.

Madagascar is also the world's biggest exporter of vanilla. The sound of the ice cream van chimes at the docks, waiting for supplies each summer's morn, is deafening.

Ice cream van congestion at Antananarivo's port.

RÉUNION

OFFICIAL NAME: Département de la Réunion (Department of Réunion)
AREA: 2,507 sq m
POPULATION: 706,300 (1999 census)
CAPITAL: Saint-Denis
LANGUAGE(S): French

In *The Rules of Popular and Rock Music*, a band cannot officially be reunited if they don't attend a "Renewing of the Rock Vows" ceremony on this French island.

MAURITIUS

OFFICIAL NAME: Republic of Mauritius
AREA: 2,040 sq km
POPULATION: 1,233,675 (2004 est.)
CAPITAL: Port Louis
LANGUAGE(S): English

Named after Earth, Wind & Fire singer Maurice White, Mauritius is one big shrine to the great man. "Boogie Wonderland" is the national anthem, and "baa dee yaa! dancing in September" is compulsory.

 MALDIVES

OFFICIAL NAME: Dhivehi Raajjeyge Jumhooriyyaa (Republic of Maldives)
AREA: 298 sq km
POPULATION: 270,101 (2000 census)
CAPITAL: Male
LANGUAGE(S): Divehi

A long, long time ago, the main island of what is now the Maldives was ruled by frogs. Tired of being made fun of by the locals who'd crouch on the ground and jump up and down making funny burping noises, the frogs ganged up and attacked. It was messy. For many years the frogs were alone on the island, then a bloke came along with a lovely princess whom he wanted to marry. She was called Princess Rebecca. When you include her royal title, she was called Princess Princess Rebecca. The good lady didn't like frogs, so the bloke put them all on a boat, hoisted the sail, and let them drift off. (The frogs eventually touched on land again some four months later when their boat came ashore, ironically enough, in France.)

Then the princess got a bit bored of living on a rubbish island and went back home to Milwaukee. The bloke was heartbroken. He cried and cried and cried. Then he cried some more. And a bit more. Then a little bit more. And again, more. And just a touch more. Then he fell asleep. When he woke up, the salt from his tears had solidified into twenty-six atolls. So he built a shitload of hotels, and now he's loaded.

 BRITISH INDIAN OCEAN TERRITORY

OFFICIAL NAME: British Indian Ocean Territory
AREA: 60 sq km
POPULATION: 4,000 (2004 est.)
CAPITAL: none
LANGUAGE(S): English

Imperial ennui was setting in by the time the Brits saw these islands. A captain of one of Her Majesty's ships lazily pointed out the window and told his cartographer to "draw them and write something next to it," before slipping below deck to cut his toenails.

 CHRISTMAS ISLAND

OFFICIAL NAME: Territory of Christmas Island
AREA: 135 sq km
POPULATION: 1,508 (2001 census)
CAPITAL: The Settlement
LANGUAGE(S): English, Chinese, Malay

Every single one of the 1,500 or so inhabitants of this island is sick to death of the song "Jingle Bells."[46]

 COCOS (KEELING) ISLANDS

OFFICIAL NAME: Territory of Cocos (Keeling) Islands
AREA: 14.2 sq km
POPULATION: 574 (2006 est.)
CAPITAL: West Island
LANGUAGE(S): Malay, English

The Cocos (Keeling) Islands are halfway between India and Australia, and are slowly disappearing. Not because of global warming or tsunami-type stuff, but because French entertainer Michel Lotito (aka Monsieur Mangetout) is eating all the atolls.

. . .

Other tiny bits of rocks in the Indian Ocean include a smattering around Madagascar that belong to France called *Îles éparses de l'océan indien* ("Scattered Islands in the Indian Ocean"—a vaguer name, even, than British Indian Ocean Territories); a couple way down south run by South Africa (Prince Edward Islands); and a bunch more in the southern bit of the ocean called the French Southern Territories, which are next to a couple of Australian bits called the Heard and McDonald Islands. The Australians also have a couple more just south of Indonesia called the Ashmore and Cartier Islands. India has some, too, in the Bay of Bengal (Andaman Islands and Nicobar Islands). British colonialists remain pissed off that they missed out on all of these islands.

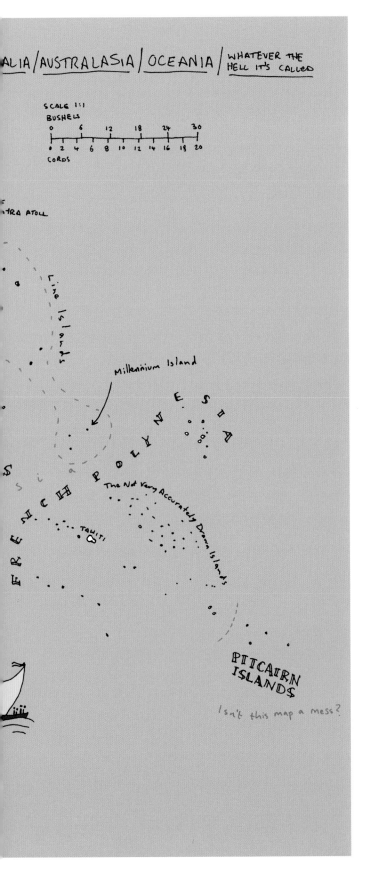

ALIA / AUSTRALASIA / OCEANIA / WHATEVER THE HELL IT'S CALLED

SCALE 1:1
BUSHELS
0   6   12   18   24   30
2 4 6 8 10 12 14 16 18 20
CORDS

...TRA ATOLL

Millennium Island

P O L Y N E S I A

FRENCH POLYNESIA

The Not Very Accurately Drawn Islands

TAHITI

PITCAIRN ISLANDS

Isn't this map a mess?

AUSTRALIA aka AUSTRALASIA aka OCEANIA

Oh gosh, can someone please decide what we're gonna call this part of the world?

Let's try and clear things up: Australia, the continent, consists of Australia, Tasmania, New Guinea, and the little islands in between. Australasia seems to add New Zealand and some of the Pacific islands. Oceania is mainly all the Pacific islands, but sometimes people include Australia and all the other bits. *Dios mio!* Those Pacific islands are split into four subregions: Melanesia is the bit east of New Guinea, Micronesia is the bit above Melanesia, Polynesia is the bit that extends in the direction of Chile, and (I apologise for this terrible joke) I forget where Amnesia is.

Whenever I think of the migration of humans from Africa to other bits of the planet, those that got to the Pacific islands make my brain tingle with joy. Just think about it—how much effort was it for humans to even get to Europe or what is now the Americas across the bit of land that used to connect Russia and Alaska? And then think about the people who set off into the unknown waters of the Pacific, hoping to find something somewhere. It fries my brain. Especially when you think of the untold horrors that must've been part of that effort, only to have Johnny European come along and start treating you like poo.

AUSTRALIA

OFFICIAL NAME: Commonwealth of Australia
AREA: 7,692,208 sq km
POPULATION: 20,293,087 (2005 est.)
CAPITAL: Canberra
LANGUAGE(S): English (de facto)

Famous for its XXXX-ing funny beer commercials, nonstop beach parties, hats with corks dangling from them, Kylie, and cricket players with moustaches and/or fluorescent sunscreen, Australia is a pretty darned big island situated a bit up from Antarctica, about a third of the way to Japan.

Australia was invented by Queen Victoria one day when she was a bit bored and thought that there weren't enough parts of the world that she owned, so she called upon England's great and good builders to make an especially big and bleak island "as far away as fucking possible." Figuring there'd be some more contracting work once the basics were done, the engineers and construction workers decided to have a nice area for themselves next to all the deserty stuff, and they named it after Her Majesty's favourite peacock, Sydney.

Australia is also known for its made-up wildlife. There's a bouncy thing called a kangaroo, and another inspired by a cartoon character called the Tasmanian Devil. A third, the koala, was manufactured by Japanese toymakers when research found that nobody thought kangaroos were "really, *really* cute."

The most impressivest thing about Australia is called Uluru (Ayers Rock). It's big, red, and in the middle of nowhere. If you can't be arsed to go—and frankly, who'd blame you—just cut a potato in half lengthways, cover it with paprika, and put it in your cat litter tray. Then stare at its majestic beauty.

A typical afternoon in Australia.

Prominent Australians include ace rock band AC/DC; chunky cricket player Merv Hughes; Paul Hogan as Crocodile Dundee; man-dressed-as-woman Dame Edna Everage; Eric Bana as Mark Brandon "Chopper" Read in Chopper; *mmmm, it's lovely Kylie Minogue; big scary Goth Nick Cave; ex-beard Nicole Kidman; big-footed swimmer Ian Thorpe; and useless indie band the Vines.*

NORFOLK ISLAND

OFFICIAL NAME: Territory of Norfolk Island
AREA: 34.6 sq km
POPULATION: 1,841 (2004 est.)
CAPITAL: Kingston
LANGUAGE(S): English, Norfuk

First sighted by Captain James Cook in 1774, the island was named after the Duchess of Norfolk because Cook thought that she was flirting with him before he set off on his journey, and he figured this naming-an-island-after-her lark might kick things up a notch. Little did he know that she was already dead by the time he'd named the place.

When he found out, he tried to change the name on the map so he could get in the Duchess of Suffolk's knickers, but he'd done the map with a marker pen, and Wite-Out hadn't been invented yet, so his luck was out.

NEW ZEALAND

OFFICIAL NAME: New Zealand/Aotearoa
AREA: 270,534 sq km
POPULATION: 4,098,260 (2005 est.)
CAPITAL: Wellington
LANGUAGE(S): English, Maori, New Zealand Sign Language

New Zealand was one of the last bits of the planet to be settled. The Polynesian ancestors of the Maori were first to arrive; then a few hundred years later, Dutchman Abel Tasman and his mates came along, had a bit of a fight, made a map, and then left again.

Some time later, the Brits piled in, had some fall-outs with the locals, made up with them, and eventually became an independent nation in 1947.

By this point, New Zealand was looking a bit worn and mucky around the edges (what with all the rugby), so they hired Peter Jackson, who swiftly painted everything blue, then CGI-ed in a newer, more beautiful background.

Melanesia

PAPUA NEW GUINEA

OFFICIAL NAME: Independent State of Papua New Guinea
AREA: 462,840 sq km
POPULATION: 5,190,786 (2000 census)
CAPITAL: Port Moresby
LANGUAGE(S): English

Papua New Guinea is the western half of the island of New Guinea, nowhere near the Gulf of Guinea, with nothing to do with Guinea, which used to be called French Guinea; or Equatorial Guinea, which used to be called Spanish Guinea; or Guinea-Bissau, which used to be called Portuguese Guinea. It's not the native land of the guinea pig or the White-breasted Guineafowl or the Black Guineafowl or the Helmeted Guineafowl or the Plumed Guineafowl or the Crested Guineafowl or even the Vulturine Guineafowl. Nor is the currency the guinea. And any Italians on holiday here would be offended if you called them Spanish.

SOLOMON ISLANDS

OFFICIAL NAME: Solomon Islands
AREA: 28,370 sq km
POPULATION: 409,042 (1999 census)
CAPITAL: Honiara
LANGUAGE(S): English

The world's oceans wouldn't be salty if it wasn't for the nine hundred "salters" from the Solomon Islands. It's their job to shake salt shakers all day to keep the oceans' salinity up.

VANUATU

OFFICIAL NAME: Ripablik blong Vanuatu/République de Vanuatu/ Republic of Vanuatu
AREA: 12,190 sq km
POPULATION: 195,444 (2001 est.)
CAPITAL: Vila
LANGUAGE(S): Bislama, French, English

On their way home from snagging French Polynesia, a couple of Gallic colonialists, Pierre et Jacques, saw this bunch of islands. Pierre exclaimed, "Sacré bleu! These islands are right tasty lookin'! Full steam ahead!" He sent Jacques down to the flag room to get another *tricolore*.

Little did they realise that coming towards Vanuatu from a slightly different angle was an English vessel. Enjoying a nice cup of tea, Peter and James spied the same pristine island. Peter exclaimed, "Bloomin' heck! Those islands there look simply lovely! Full steam ahead!" He sent James down to the flag room to get another Union Jack. Once James had gone below deck, Peter gestured impatiently to a nearby lad, "Boatswain, come hither and polish my shoes at once. And be sure to do a capital job or I'll see to it that you're killed."

At the exact same moment, Pierre et Jacques and Peter and James jumped off their boats and whacked their flags into the sand. "Merde!" cried Pierre. "Oh, bother!" moaned Peter. Pierre and Peter started pushing each other around like school children preparing to fight in the playground.

While all this went on, Jacques and James sat down and worked out a plan whereby they could share the islands. Four hours of negotiations later, the New Hebrides (as Vanuatu came to be known) was ruled jointly by the French and English. A quick ceremonial photograph was taken place before Jacques and James stepped in to stop Pierre and Peter pushing each other around. They spent the next few weeks betting on which of the volcanoes on some of the eighty-three islands would erupt next.

In 1980, the islands gained independence and changed their name to Vanuatu. They still like betting on the volcanoes, though.

Jacques and James sort stuff out.

NEW CALEDONIA

OFFICIAL NAME: Nouvelle-Calédonia (New Caledonia)
AREA: 18,575 sq km
POPULATION: 230,789 (2004 census)
CAPITAL: Nouméa
LANGUAGE(S): French

An overseas bit of France, New Caledonia is apparently "France's best kept secret."

So secret, in fact, that when I telephoned the island's mayor Willy McTartan to ask him about it, he replied, "Fuck off! French!? Ye gotta be fuckin' kidding me!" before slamming down the phone to play his bagpipes.

FIJI

OFFICIAL NAME: Republic of the Fiji Islands/Kai Vakarairai ni Fiji
AREA: 18,272 sq km
POPULATION: 775,077 (1996 census)
CAPITAL: Suva
LANGUAGE(S): English, Fijian, Hundustani (Fijian Hindi)

Rugby union is the national sport of Fiji. All the tough guys play it. But there was one boy, let's call him Mark Hooper (not his real name), who was not very good at rugby. All the kids picked on him at school, pushing him around and jeering and shouting, "Mark Pooper! Mark Pooper! You're not super-duper!" This would make Mark sad. And he would cry. Big, fat, salty tears of dejection. He'd walk along the Waisalima beach, head hung low, wishing he could play rugby like the other lads. "It's not fair, nothing ever goes right for me," he muttered to himself, as a coconut fell on his head.

Micronesia

PALAU

OFFICIAL NAME: Belu'u er a Belau/Republic of Palau
AREA: 488 sq km
POPULATION: 19,129 (2000 census)
CAPITAL: Melekeok
LANGUAGE(S): Palauan, English

One of the world's youngest nations (gained independence in 1994), Palau still gets a lollipop if it's been a good girl at the dentist's.

MICRONESIA

OFFICIAL NAME: Federated States of Micronesia
AREA: 701.4 sq km
POPULATION: 107,008 (2000 census)
CAPITAL: Palikir, on Pohnpei
LANGUAGE(S): English, Ulithian, Woleaian, Yapese, Phonpeian, Kosraean, Chuukese

If you took a map of the Federated States of Micronesia and joined the dots, it'd look like a swordfish. Or maybe a cheetah running at full speed. Or a really tall kangaroo extending its neck to try to win the hundred metres at the Olympics.

GUAM

OFFICIAL NAME: Teritorion Guam/Territory of Guam
AREA: 541 sq km
POPULATION: 154,805 (2000 census)
CAPITAL: Hagåtña
LANGUAGE(S): Chamorro

There are more snakes in Guam than at a Gorgon sister's birthday party. This wasn't always the case; once upon a time there were no snakes. Golden days for the birds of Guam, they were. Frolicking on the beach, catching inflatable balls between their wings, having worm barbeques, playing Pictionary… Then one day, a ship arrived from the U.S. and off slunk some brown tree snakes. Feathers everywhere. Carnage.

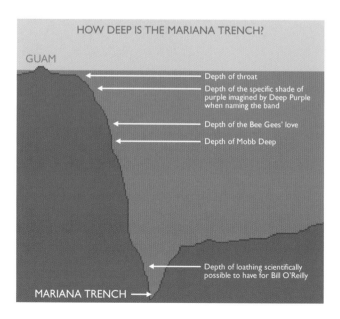

HOW DEEP IS THE MARIANA TRENCH?

GUAM

Depth of throat

Depth of the specific shade of purple imagined by Deep Purple when naming the band

Depth of the Bee Gees' love

Depth of Mobb Deep

Depth of loathing scientifically possible to have for Bill O'Reilly

MARIANA TRENCH →

 NORTHERN MARIANA ISLANDS

OFFICIAL NAME: Commonwealth of the Northern Mariana Islands
AREA: 457.1 sq km
POPULATION: 69,221 (2000 census)
CAPITAL: Saipan
LANGUAGE(S): Chamorro, Carolinia, English

There's nothing more the good folks of the U.S. territory of the Northern Mariana Islands like better than the national hobby of "sauna stitching." This involves going into a really hot room and making clothes. They love it! They don't really want payment for it—it's so much fun!—but, not wanting to be rude, they keep the few cents flipped in their direction and spend it on food for their children.[47]

 WAKE ISLAND

OFFICIAL NAME: Wake Island
AREA: 6.5 sq km
POPULATION: no indigenous inhabitants, 200 contractor personnel (2006 est.)
CAPITAL: none
LANGUAGE(S): whatever the contractors speak

Wake Island is actually three small atolls very close together that have been annexed by the U.S. since 1899. Not much has gone on there because of the wake. No records are available detailing who died exactly, but the wake's been going on for ages, and no one dares ask because the widow still keeps making lovely sandwiches and there's plenty of whiskey.

 MARSHALL ISLANDS

OFFICIAL NAME: Majōl/Republic of the Marshall Islands
AREA: 181.43 sq km
POPULATION: 50,848 (1999 census)
CAPITAL: Majuro (local name is DUD [acronym of Delap, Uliga, and Djarrit])
LANGUAGE(S): Marshallese (Kajin-Majōl), English

Fully independent since 1990, the Marshall Islands is a nation consisting of five islands and twenty-nine atolls. Prior to that, it was one of the many Pacific bits snaffled up by the United States. The most famous part of the Marshall Islands is Bikini Atoll, where the U.S. did some nuclear testing. They'd not decided which atoll to do it on, but then they noticed two men on Bikini Atoll discussing the idea of getting married to each other and decided to teach them a lesson.

The gays about to kiss each other on the beach of Bikini Atoll, triggering the release of an atomic bomb.

NAURU

OFFICIAL NAME: Naoero (Republic of Nauru)
AREA: 21.2 sq km
POPULATION: 9,919 (1992 census)
CAPITAL: none (government offices in Yaren District)
LANGUAGE(S): Nauruan, English

This island, a bit east of Papua New Guinea, used to be called Pleasant Island. The name of the island was changed after an infamous event known as Unpleasant Day.

After a hard day's phosphate mining, an argument broke out in a pub about which town should be Pleasant Island's capital. Two blokes had had a couple too many and started duffing each other up in the car park. One of them sprained his ankle when he fell over a curb and the other lost a fingernail. The other islanders were shocked and appalled. They vowed never to have a capital city.

KIRIBATI

OFFICIAL NAME: Republic of Kiribati
AREA: 810.5 sq km
POPULATION: 84,494 (2000 census)
CAPITAL: South Tarawa
LANGUAGE(S): English, Kiribati

After watching the Americans at Bikini Atoll, the Brits decided to have a pop at nuclear testing. They couldn't find any homosexuals to punish but they saw a very disorderly queue outside a telephone kiosk on Kiritimati which, frankly, deserved nothing less than some H-bomb kisses.

Polynesia

TUVALU

OFFICIAL NAME: Tuvalu
AREA: 25.63 sq km
POPULATION: 9,561 (2002 census)
CAPITAL: Vaiaku
LANGUAGE(S): Tuvaluan, English

Our splendid British explorers Peter and James had heard the tales of other colonialists getting close to, but never landing on, the Pacific island nation of Tuvalu and took it as a challenge. "Damn Johnny Foreigner's eyes, James! Those perfectly useless atolls will be ours!" said Peter. So off they set on another journey, intent on making sure a nation of happy brown people began living life in a purer Christian manner.

After converting people and drinking all their water, Peter and James got bored and went home. Nowadays Tuvalu—the fourth smallest country in the world—is, quite frankly, up shit creek. You see, most of Tuvalu's land is only a few metres above sea level, so climate change is likely to—sooner or later—make the whole of Tuvalu look like a child's paddling pool. The land is sinking, too, just to make things worse. So go and turn your telly off now, rather than leaving it sucking up electricity on standby.

WALLIS and FUTUNA

OFFICIAL NAME: Territoire de Wallis et Futuna (Territory of Wallis and Futuna Islands)
AREA: 274 sq km
POPULATION: 15,480 (2005 est.)
CAPITAL: Mata-Utu
LANGUAGE(S): French, Wallisian, Futunian

The islands of Wallis and Futuna were first discovered in the mid-nineteenth century by two European music-hall entertainers, "Jumpin'" Jack Wallis and "Laughin'" Larry Futuna. They were originally the entertainers on a cruise ship, but the passengers and crew soon tired of their puppetry, songs about life in Cockney London, rubbish jokes, and deadly knife-throwing act.

After one particularly nasty fire-eating accident that singed the captain's majestic eyebrows, they were thrown overboard and drifted apart to the atolls to which they gave their names.

Much like the nation's founders, Wallisians and Futunans still gather around beach fires to have a good singsong, before the mayor closes proceedings with a bit of juggling and his tear-jerking rendition of "I Left Me Undershirt on Mrs. Cartwright's Banister."

TOKELAU

OFFICIAL NAME: Tokelau
AREA: 10 sq km
POPULATION: 1,378 (2005 est.)
CAPITAL: none (each of the three atolls has its own administrative centre)
LANGUAGE(S): Tokelauan, English

With virtually no land more than two metres above sea level, the people of Tokelau (the atolls of Atafu, Nukunonu, and Fakaofo) are all learning how to walk on stilts.

SAMOA

OFFICIAL NAME: Malo Sa'oloto Tuto'atasi o Samoa/Independent State of Samoa
AREA: 2,831 sq km
POPULATION: 176,710 (2001 census)
CAPITAL: Apia
LANGUAGE(S): Samoan, English

This bunch of islands used to be known as Navigators Islands due to the number of natives who stood on the beach dressed in fluorescent bibs, helping ships find other Polynesian islands, and handing out parking permits.

A friendly Samoan chap giving some directions to a lost pirate.

AMERICAN SAMOA

OFFICIAL NAME: American Samoa/Amerika Samoa
AREA: 218 sq km
POPULATION: 57,291 (2000 census)
CAPITAL: Fagatogo (legislative and judicial) and Utulei (executive)
LANGUAGE(S): English, Samoan

Same as Samoa, just with more flavours of bubble gum.

TONGA

OFFICIAL NAME: Pule'anga Fakatu'i 'o Tonga/Kingdom of Tonga
AREA: 750 sq km
POPULATION: 97,784 (1996 census)
CAPITAL: Nuku'alofa
LANGUAGE(S): Tongan, English

Captain Cook stopped off here on several of his jaunts. He liked Tonga and often picked up his duty-free gifts here. On one of his trips he'd forgotten to bring some presents for his Tongan mates, so he had a think and a rummage around his cabin, and grabbed one of the tortoises he'd got in Madagascar.

"It's not much, and I really don't know how it works," he said, offering the tortoise to the king. "I think it's a toy of some sort, but there's nowhere to put the batteries, and I can't find the thing that winds it up…but, y'know, it looks kind of interesting, huh? Maybe you could use it as a paperweight…."

The king accepted the gift, gave it some lettuce, and named it Tu'i Malila.

Tu'i Malila lived to be 188 years old, probably the longest-living animal ever. She even met Queen Elizabeth II in 1953, who remarked, "Oh, how charming! Philip, look! A paperweight!"

NIUE

OFFICIAL NAME: Niue
AREA: 260 sq km
POPULATION: 1,445 (2005 est.)
CAPITAL: Alofi
LANGUAGE(S): Niuean, English

There's a rock on Niue and it's nothing special to look at. Just a rock near some trees. But if you look really hard, you'll see a little button on the ground. If you were to press that button, the rock would move and you'd see a tunnel that goes all the way to northern Niger on the opposite side of the planet. Saves on plane tickets, see.

COOK ISLANDS

OFFICIAL NAME: Cook Islands/ Kūki 'Āiran
AREA: 240 sq km
POPULATION: 17,954 (2005 est.)
CAPITAL: Avarua
LANGUAGE(S): English, Cook Islands Maori

Unsurprisingly, named after Captain James Cook. He was on his first voyage to the Pacific Ocean, and having already given lots of islands names of royalty, his rich pals, and some ladies he fancied, he looked out at these fifteen small islands and pondered aloud, "What shall we call these pretty fellows, eh?" Several members of his crew umm-ed and aah-ed, while Cook sauntered over to the handsome portrait of himself and casually pointed at it whilst fiddling with his breastful of medals.

"Erm, what about the Cook Islands, captain?" said one of the crew, his voice full to the brim with obsequiousness.

Cook feigned modesty and blustered, "Wha? Well, erm, I don't know…very nice of you to suggest it, but…"

"Okay, what about the Pretty Islands?" suggested someone else.

Slightly irked, Cook backtracked, "Well, Cook Islands does have a certain *je ne sais quoi*, doesn't it…? Yes, I like it! Cook Islands it is!"

And with that, he went to his cabin to try and get one of those darned tortoises to work properly.

FRENCH POLYNESIA

OFFICIAL NAME: Polynésie française/Polynesia Farani (French Polynesia)
AREA: 4,000 sq km
POPULATION: 245,516 (2002 census)
CAPITAL: Papeete
LANGUAGE(S): French, Tahitian

French Polynesia aren't real islands; they're floating platforms, a bit like those plastic things that separate the lanes in swimming pools. As the name suggests, the islands were annexed by the French in the nineteenth century. Our intrepid Frenchy colonialists Pierre et Jacques were the first to set foot on one of the islands (Tahiti) and tricked the locals into signing over their land. They got some perfumed ladies to flash their ding-dongs while doing the cancan. Never having seen nipple tassles before, the locals were hypnotised. While in this state, Pierre et Jacques whipped out the contracts, got the locals to sign them, and skipped off backstage where they were pleasured at great length by the petticoat-wearing dancing girls.

Having acquired Polynesia and slapped the word "French" on the front, Pierre et Jacques went off again on a new adventure, forgetting, however, to click their fingers to wake the locals from their hypnotic state. Not until a tourist turned on a telly and began watching *The*

A teeny-weeny bang in someone's back yard.

Addams Family did they awaken. Annoyed by the dastardly tricks played on them, the locals kicked off and went a bit mental, breaking chairs, squashing fruit, and such. As soon as word got back to Paris, the French hit upon a way to quieten things down—testing nuclear weapons in the Polynesians' back gardens. The locals soon shut up and got back to posing for European painters.

PITCAIRN ISLANDS

OFFICIAL NAME: Pitcairn, Henderson, Ducie, and Oeno Islands
AREA: 5 sq km
POPULATION: 47 (2006, I'm guessing they didn't need a census)
CAPITAL: Adamstown
LANGUAGE(S): English, Pitkern

Famously, the Pitcairn Island is the place where Fletcher Christian and his fellow *Bounty* mutineers settled after bunging William Bligh off the ship. The fate of Christian should serve as a warning to all shitty bosses across the world: He was murdered by the Tahitians whom he'd been treating like slaves.

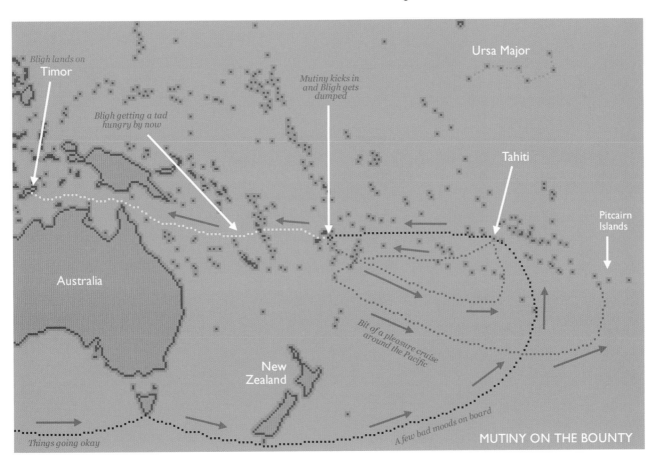

MUTINY ON THE BOUNTY

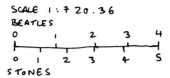

MAP of THE PACIFIC OCEAN

SCALE 1 : 7 20.36
BEATLES

0   1   2   3   4

0   1   2   3   4   S
STONES

North America

CLIPPERTON IS.

GALAPAGOS IS.

ISLA DE LOS
DESVENTURADOS

EASTER
ISLAND

ISLA JAUN
FERNANDEZ

erel I ISLAND

PACIFIC OCEAN

Oooh, it's a big old lake this one. It takes up about a third of the surface of the planet. I bet property developers would make a mess in their trousers if we decided to drain the water out. The ocean extends from the eastern coast of Asia and down past the splatter of southeast Asian islands and Australia all the way to the Americas on the other side.

It's got some plates underneath it that are moving about, slowly creating trenches and stuff.

The name of the ocean comes from Latin, meaning "peaceful sea," which kinda ignores all the earthquakes and volcanoes that go on around the rim of the ocean. And it ignores the wave machine that the Japanese put in the ocean in 1986.

As for land in the Pacific Ocean, there's an estimated twenty thousand to thirty thousand islands. If the deadline for finishing this book was September 2014, I'd list them all. It's not though, and so I won't.

As well as the islands of Oceania, there are some Japanese islands, the Aleutian Islands of Alaska, a couple of Russian ones, the Philippines, Tracy Island (home of International Rescue), and Indonesia. There are also some American bits and bobs: Hawaii, the fiftieth state; and a bunch of islands collectively titled the United States Minor Outlying Islands (which, oddly, also includes Navassa Island in the Caribbean). Those Minor Outlying Islands (minus Navassa Island) are also known as the United States Pacific Island Wildlife Refuges. This is where the U.S. government is putting all the wildlife it "owns" so it can get on with polluting the world without those hippy environmentalists getting all weepy and annoying.

There are a couple of bits in the Pacific Ocean that warrant further examination....

EASTER ISLAND

OFFICIAL NAME: Rapu Nui (Big Rapa)/Isla da Pascua (Passover Island)
AREA: 163.6 sq km
POPULATION: 3,791 (2005 est.)
CAPITAL: Hanga Roa
LANGUAGE(S): Rapa Nui, Spanish

About a third of the way from the Pitcairn Islands to Chile is Easter Island, which is fairly remote by any standards of remoteness. Yet there's still a bunch of people who live there, and a fair few tourists, too. They mainly go to see the *moai* (the **887** big stone statue things along the coast). The *moai* have been around since about 1000 AD.

Archaeologists believe that the very first *moai* was carved by a boyfriend-less teenage girl named Tiffany. Cave paintings depict a slightly plain girl with two other people playing pool. The slightly plain girl is staring mournfully into her alcopop while the other two figures are snogging against the pool table. The depiction of the slightly plain girl's expression can possibly be interpreted as her wondering if she'll ever get a boyfriend, wondering why she bothered to come and play pool when all she ever does is sit and watch them snogging all the time, and wondering what life would be like if only her boobs were as big as Melissa's. Further cave paintings show a similarly plain girl carving, and subsequently posing with, a *moai*. The accepted theory is that the slightly plain girl carved the *moai* so she could have a boy of her own, one that she could talk to and sit with, watching the sun setting over the sea.

Tiffany cuddlin' with her moai, *Ricky.*

GALÁPOGOS ISLANDS

OFFICIAL NAME: Archipiélago de Colón (Columbus Archipelago)
AREA: 8,010 sq km
POPULATION: 18,000 (2006 est.)
CAPITAL: Puerto Baquerizo Moreno
LANGUAGE(S): Spanish

The Galápogos Islands is a province of Ecuador, nearly a thousand miles west of the mainland. Its very existence really winds up creationists. All those different creatures evolving to be different on each of the islands…that's gotta really hurt their brains. It was here, of course, that Charles Darwin began to connect the dots and think that maybe this God-created-everything-in-less-than-a-week stuff was a crock of shit. Well done, Charles. Well done, tortoises. Well done, nature, for creating something so mind-blowingly beautiful as evolution.

BIT AT THE END

So, that's the planet we live on. It's not all true of course. A lot of the things you've just read are jokes or lies for comedic value. There is, though, also a lot of truth and facts in there.

Sadly, we humans have probably been the worst thing that has happened to the world.

We're using up the world's resources at an alarming rate and the planet's getting way too hot. We've managed to endanger many species of plants and animals in a pretty short space of time. And we have the methods to get rid of every last one of them—including ourselves—should that be the wish of a few power-crazed idiots.

We, and by this I mainly mean Europeans, Americans, and other westerners, all have ancestors who've fucked over people on other continents for their own benefit. We're a sorry bunch.

But we have also shown we can be great. That's obvious in the music of Mozart and Brian Wilson, the art of Yves Klein and Mark Rothko, the writing of F. Scott Fitzgerald and Harper Lee, the skills of Zinedine Zidane and Diego Maradona, and the incredible ideas of Albert Einstein and Sir Isaac Newton.

There's the ability of our friends and loved ones to make us laugh, to say the right words when we're feeling down, and to give us a hug when we need it most.

We can expand on this, and do it for everyone. There are more of us good people than the few evil fuckers in power. We can take them! It's a cliché, but every little bit helps, whether it's giving your time to a charity, sponsoring a child in a far-flung corner of the world, or simply picking up the apples that an old lady's dropped on her way home from the shops.

It's a beautiful world and we're all here *right now*.

Cool, huh?

NOTES

1. It's not really about you, I'm just saying that to be nice. (Unless you are Hitler or Stalin, then bits of it *are* about you. And I wouldn't really be bothering to try to be nice to you two, even if you weren't mentioned.)

2. This is no joke. I got a D grade in my O level. Even so, my school didn't take that as a bad sign; they still let me do a Geography A level, which I proceeded to mess up pretty badly, eventually achieving a U grade, which stands for "ungraded," i.e., utterly crap.

3. *Planet Earth* and *The Blue Planet* are also excellent BBC natural history documentaries.

4. You might actually wanna skip the whole book, really. Note how I tell you this in the notes, not in the introduction. I may think your cult is a bit silly but I still want your money.

5. I've been on a small boat on the river that forms part of the border between Mexico and Guatemala. It was a wonderful experience despite the French guy on the boat who wouldn't stop talking. I saw a crocodile in that river too, which was one of the best moments of my life.

6. My favourite Slush Puppie is the blue one. They always remind me of being a pre-teen, going swimming at Yarborough Leisure Centre in Lincoln. It was my post-swim drink and a perfect complement to the bacon-flavoured crisps I'd eat.

7. Part of Greenland is called Disko Island. It's only a matter of time before there's a Stereolab song with the same name, really.

8. My other favourites: Japan, Cuba, Switzerland, Somalia, Greece, and, occasionally, Libya.

9. Mexico is also home to the world's coolest ever man: Subcomandante Marcos, the spokesperson of the Zapatista Army of National Liberation. Not only does he wear a balaclava *and* a hat, he wears multiple watches, smokes a pipe, and rides around on a black motorcycle with a rooster mascot that he calls a penguin. All while sticking it to the man. *Maravilloso!*

10. Which is exactly what I did when I visited southern Mexico, so perhaps I should stop being sarcastic.

11. Lead singer of U2, the first band I ever saw live. I've not quite decided whether I find Bono incredibly annoying or incredibly great. He seems to be able to be both quite well.

12. In the long run, Reagan was right: Nicaragua's children are the future, with almost 40 percent of Nicaragua's population under fifteen years of age.

13. Cuba looks a bit like one of those Chinese dragons they have at New Year's festivals, jumping over a comma.

14. Balloons. They blow up balloons here.

15. Keith told a lie. The Rubik's Cube was actually invented by a Hungarian chap called Erno Rubik in 1974.

16. A little known fact about the current, Bush-baiting president: Hugo Chávez used to be in his country's number-one pop group, a band called the Venez Wailers that specialised in Bob Marley covers rendered in the local Gaito style.

17. I've only ever met one person from Argentina and he laughed like an otter being strangled. Not sure if this is what all Argentinian people sound like when they laugh, but I do know that the Argentinian accent is considered *muy sexy* by most Latin American women.

18. One of the earliest uses of that word is in Chaucer's *Canterbury Tales*. In an exchange between two sailors regarding their captain, one of the sailors concurs, "Aye, you're right, mayte, he's a fuckyng cunt."

19. Apparently, he did actually try out for the Algerian team, but the coach at the time wasn't impressed.

20. Not me, I quite like it, much to my mates' amusement.

21. Djibouti is home to Africa's lowest point, Lake Assal. It's 150 metres below sea level, has no rivers flowing into it, and is, therefore, really, really salty. They should fill it with peanuts and open a bar nearby; they'd make a fortune.

22. Hitler must have been annoyed that Germany lost Tanzania before he came to power, as it's an anagram of "a Nazi tan," something he was planning to get on the beaches of Zanzibar.

23. Zambia takes its name from the Zambezi River. Zambezi's a great name, huh? I think any name with two Zs in it is always gonna be good: Zambezi, Zinedine Zidane, and ZZ Top being the only three examples I can think of.

24. Zimbabwe's first president was Canaan Banana. This, of course, is funny. Even funnier though, for some reason, is that his wife was called Janet Banana.

25. This was when Dr. David Livingstone went there and found Mosi-oa-Tunya and renamed it Victoria Falls. I've always been suspicious of Henry Morton Stanley's claim that he said "Dr. Livingstone, I presume?" It seems a bit too much like a James Bond quip for my liking.

26. Every single person from Iceland has been on television.

27. The worst instrument ever invented. No song has ever been improved by a saxophone solo. Fact. (Apart from "Jungleland" by Bruce Springsteen.)

28. The borders of Luxembourg have changed quite often, due to bits of it being annexed by France, Belgium, and Germany. The current border, established in 1839, was measured out by the grand duke standing at the top of his castle and pissing in a circle. Where the royal urine landed became the edges of his nation.

29. Is there something in the water in Austria that breeds people who like to be in charge of other parts of the world? Hitler, Schwarzenegger…and Kurt Waldheim was the UN secretary general, too.

30. Swoon!

31. I like Jean-Michel Jarre. Twenty years later, I'm still impressed by that laser harp thingy he uses.
32. I hate to praise any Manchester United player in print, but it's undeniable: Cantona was pretty good.
33. My hometown. The cathedral is lovely. You really should pay a visit.
34. If you've not seen the video, Google it—it's excellent.
35. There's a thin strip of land separating the Cyprus and Northern Cyprus bits called the Green Line which is patrolled by UN peacekeeping forces. My mum went into the Green Line area when she was on holiday and said it was "rubbish."
36. My grandmother once told me that Polish is the only English word that can have a different meaning simply by making the first letter a capital letter. Not sure if this is true or not, but I like to think she's right.
37. See also Chile (no, it's quite mild for the time of year), Jamaica (no, she came of her own free will), Russia (no, I wasn't in a hurry), and Jakarta (no, we took our bicycles).
38. Apologies for the *Star Wars* reference; I know it's quite a tedious trait of thirty-something-year-old men.
39. When I worked as a Web designer, I did some stuff for the German MTV site. Lacking inspiration and the will to work one evening, I checked out all the other MTV sites from around the world. I can say that, as of 2001, MTV India had the best-looking VJs by far.
40. That joke was far better in my head than it appears here, so, y'know, please laugh at something funny on telly and then quickly look back at the book. That'd make me happy.
41. Baseball bat manufactured by Hillerich & Bradsby. Primarily used for playing baseball, although often used to beat the shit out of people.
42. I preferred Blur.
43. This is a totally superfluous endnote. I just wanna check if you're still paying attention.
44. I hate the Doors. Never in this world has there been a more overrated band (apart from the Clash).
45. Sometimes the pride I feel for my home nation swells up in my chest and I can feel my penis rising to ejaculate a Great Britain-shaped splodge of spunk onto the carpet.
46. "Jingle Bells" was written in 1857 by James Pierpont.
47. Clothes made in the sweatshops of the Northern Mariana Islands are labelled "Made in USA."

SOURCES

Plenty of sources were used, as you'd imagine. Bits and bobs of information were found on Web sites relating to each individual country, tourism, and government sites, etc. The main sources, though, were:

BBC News. http://news.bbc.co.uk

Blainey, Geoffrey. *A Very Short History of the World.* London: Penguin/Allan Lane, 2004.

The CIA World Factbook. http://www.cia.gov/cia/publications/factbook/index.html

Encyclopædia Britannica Online. http://www.britannica.com

Heritage, Andrew, ed. *Dorling Kindersley Concise Atlas of the World.* New York: Dorling Kindersley, 2005.

Mahler, Scott, ed. *National Geographic Almanac of Geography.* Washington, D.C.: National Geographic Society, 2005.

Persuad, Tina, ed. *The Guinness Book of Answers (9th Edition).* Middlesex, UK: Guinness Publishing, 1993.

Sharp, Katie John. *My First Atlas.* Lincolnwood, Ill.: Publications International, Ltd., 2005.

Tresidder, Jack, ed. *The Hamlyn Pictorial Atlas of the World.* London: Hamlyn Publishing Group, 1977.

Wikipedia. http://www.wikipedia.org

ACKNOWLEDGMENTS

Thanks to Deborah Aaronson, Emma Anderson, John
Bassett, Becki Cook, Mark Hooper, Khrystell Jimenez
Zavaleta, Laura Lindgren, Keith McColl, Steve McLay,
Naomi Palovits, Hanni Pannier, Jacquie Poirier, Derick
Rhodes, Josh Rosen, Silke Scharunge, Mark Svartz, Laura
Tam, and Elizabeth Wright. My inability to resist telling
them useless facts about the exports of various Pacific
islands was tolerated by all of them. And they've offered
opinions that, ignored or noted, were always appreciated.

Thanks for reading my book.
I hope you enjoyed it.
And if you're flicking through from the back,
I hope you enjoy reading it.

INDEX